심청전

The Story of Sim Cheong

머리말

"다락원 한국어 학습문고" 시리즈는 대표적인 한국 문학 작품을 한국어 학습자들의 읽기 수준에 맞도록 재구성하여 쉽고 재미있게 독해력을 증진할 수 있도록 하였습니다. '국제 통용 한국어 표준 교육 과정'과 '한국어 교육 어휘 내용 개발'을 기준으로 초급부터 고급(A1~C2)으로 구분하여 지문을 읽으면서 각자의 수준에 맞는 필수 어휘와 표현을 자연스럽게 익힐 수 있습니다.

시대적 배경과 관련된 어휘에는 별도의 설명을 추가하여 그 당시 문화에 대해 이해하면서 본문을 읽을 수 있도록 하였습니다. 더불어 의미 전달에 충실한 번역문과 내용 이해 문제를 수록하여 자신의 이해 정도를 점검하고 확인할 수 있도록 하였고, 전문 성우가 직접 낭독한 음원을 통해 눈과 귀를 동시에 활용한 독해 연습이 가능하도록 하였습니다.

"다락원 한국어 학습문고" 시리즈를 통해 보다 유익하고 재미있는 한국어 학습이 되시길 바랍니다.

다락원 한국어 학습문고
저자 대표 **김유미**

Preface

The Darakwon Korean Readers series adapts the most well-known Korean literary works to the reading levels of Korean language learners, restructuring them into simple and fun stories that encourage the improvement of reading comprehension skills. Based on the "International Standard Curriculum for the Korean Language" and "Research on Korean Language Education Vocabulary Content Development", the texts have been graded from beginner to advanced levels (A1–C2) so that readers can naturally learn the necessary vocabulary and expressions that match their level.

With supplementary explanations concerning historical background, learners can understand the culture of the era as they read. In addition, students can assess and confirm their understanding with the included reading comprehension questions and translations faithful to the meaning of the original text. Recordings of the stories by professional voice actors also allow reading practice through the simultaneous use of learners' eyes and ears.

We hope that the Darakwon Korean Readers series will provide learners with a more fruitful and interesting Korean language learning experience.

Darakwon Korean Readers
Kim Yu Mi, Lead Author

일러두기

How to Use This Book

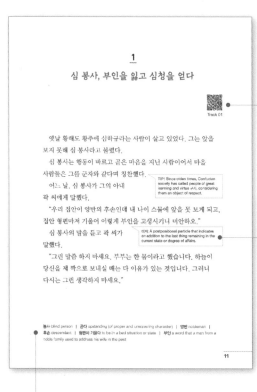

듣기 Listening

QR 코드를 통해 전문 성우가 녹음한 정확하고 생생한 작품 낭독을 들을 수 있습니다.

Using the corresponding QR codes, learners can access professional recordings of the story.

해설 Notes

학습자들이 내용을 이해하는 데 필요한 한국어 문법, 표현, 어휘, 속담, 문화적 배경 등을 알기 쉽게 설명해 주어 별도로 사전을 찾을 필요가 없도록 하였습니다.

Explanations of essential Korean grammar, expressions, vocabulary, proverbs, cultural background, etc. are provided to learners to aid understanding without the need to consult a separate dictionary.

어휘 설명 Vocabulary Explanation

각 권의 수준에 맞춰 본문에서 꼭 알아야 하는 필수 어휘를 영어 번역과 함께 제시하였습니다.

English translations are provided for the essential vocabulary matched to the level of each title.

내용 이해하기 Reading Comprehension

다양한 문제를 통해 본문 내용 이해와 함께 해당 레벨에서 알아야 할 문형과 어휘를 다시 한번 확인할 수 있습니다.

Learners can check their understanding of the main text while also reviewing the essential sentence patterns and vocabulary for their level through various comprehension questions.

본문 번역 Text Translations

한국어 본문 내용을 정확히 이해할 수 있도록 의미 전달에 충실한 영어 번역을 수록하였습니다.

An English translation faithful to the original text is included to ensure an exact understanding of the original Korean story.

모범 답안 Answers

모범 답안과 비교하며 자신의 이해 정도를 스스로 평가하고 진단할 수 있습니다.

Learners can self-evaluate and assess their level of understanding by comparing their answers to the answer key.

작품 소개

심청전

"심청전"은 한국의 대표적인 고전 소설입니다. 지은이가 누구인지, 창작 시기가 정확히 언제인지는 알 수 없지만, 조선 시대에 한글로 쓰인 것으로 추측됩니다. 오랜 시간 사람들의 입에서 입으로 전해 내려온 만큼, 심청전에는 당시 사람들이 중요하게 여겼던 가치가 반영되어 있다고 할 수 있습니다.

"심청전"은 눈먼 아버지의 눈을 뜨게 하기 위해 자신을 희생한 심청의 이야기를 다루고 있는 작품으로, '효'를 중요시했던 조선 시대의 분위기를 그대로 반영하고 있습니다. 한국에서는 예로부터 부모에게 효도하는 것을 나라의 근본이자 인간이 반드시 추구해야 하는 기본 가치로 여겼습니다. 효를 권장하기 위해 효심이 깊은 사람에게 상을 내리거나 기념비를 세워 주고, 관리로 뽑기도 했습니다. 뿐만 아니라 효성스러운 사람들의 이야기를 모아 엮거나 효가 무엇인지 알 수 있게 하는 책을 만들어 나누어 주기도 했습니다.

"심청전"에서는 심청의 효를 통해 보통 사람의 힘으로는 해결하기 어려운 일들이 해결되는 모습이 나타납니다. 그런데 심청이 아버지를 위해 했던 일을 현대적인 관점에서는 진정한 효라고 볼 수 있는지 의문과 비판이 제기되기도 합니다. 효에 대한 관점 역시 시대에 따라 변화하기 때문입니다. "심청전"을 읽으면서 심청의 선택과 그 선택에 담긴 의미를 생각해 보고, 진정한 효란 무엇인지 생각해 봅시다.

Introduction to the Story

The Story of Sim Cheong

"The Story of Sim Cheong" is a representative classic Korean tale. While we cannot know precisely who wrote it or when it was written, it is speculated to have been written in Hangeul during the Joseon dynasty. As it traveled by word of mouth for a long time, we can say that "The Story of Sim Cheong" reflects the values that were important to people at the time.

As "The Story of Sim Cheong" is about Sim Cheong, who sacrifices herself so that her blind father's sight can be restored, it accurately reflects the atmosphere of the Joseon dynasty, which placed great importance on filial duty. Since the olden days in Korea, serving one's parents with devotion has been considered both fundamental to the country and a basic value that a human being must necessarily pursue. In order to encourage filial devotion, those who were deeply dutiful to their parents would be handed down a prize or have a monument erected in their honor, and were even recruited into the government. And this is not all; the stories of dutiful people were collected and compiled, and books were made and distributed so that people could know what filial duty was.

In "The Story of Sim Cheong," Sim Cheong is presented as using her filial devotion to solve difficult problems that cannot be solved by the strength of ordinary people. But from a modern day perspective, questions and criticisms are raised as to whether the things that Sim Cheong did for her father could be called genuine filial duty. This is because, as expected, our view of filial duty changes with the times. While reading "The Story of Sim Cheong," try thinking about Sim Cheong's choice and the meaning infused in that choice, as well as what true filial devotion is.

목차

Table of Contents

심청전

The Story of Sim Cheong

등장인물
Characters

심청
Sim Cheong

마음씨 착한 딸이다. 자신을 어렵게 키워 준 눈먼 아버지를 위해 목숨까지 내놓는다.

A good-hearted daughter. She gives her life for her blind father who raised her with difficulty.

심학규
Sim Hakkyu

심청의 아버지이다. 앞을 못 보는 맹인으로 부인이 일찍 죽어 혼자 어린 딸을 키운다.

Sim Cheong's father. A blind man. His wife dies early on and he raises his young daughter by himself.

곽 씨
Ms. Gwak

심청이의 어머니이다. 맹인인 심학규를 대신해 집안일을 한다. 심청을 낳고 칠일 만에 죽는다.

Sim Cheong's mother. She takes care of the household affairs in place of the blind Sim Hakkyu. She dies just seven days after giving birth to Sim Cheong.

옥진 부인
Lady Okjin

곽 씨가 하늘나라의 신선이 된 모습이다. 옥황상제의 허락을 받아 용궁에 있는 심청을 만나게 된다.

The form Ms. Gwak takes as she becomes an Taoist hermit in heaven. She receives permission from the Great Jade Emperor and meets Sim Cheong, who is in the Dragon Palace.

황제
The Emperor

이 나라의 임금으로, 심청을 황후로 맞이한다. 심청의 고민을 들은 뒤 심청의 아버지를 찾아 주려고 노력한다.

The ruler of this country, he receives Sim Cheong as the Empress. After hearing Sim Cheong's worries, he tries to find her father for her.

뺑덕 어미
Bbaengdeok's Mother

심봉사가 심청이 떠난 뒤 얻은 아내이다. 게으르고 욕심 많은 사람으로, 심 봉사의 재산을 다 써 버리고 도망간다.

The wife of Blind Man Sim after Sim Cheong leaves. A lazy and greedy person, she uses up all of Blind Man Sim's fortune and then runs away.

1

심 봉사, 부인을 잃고 심청을 얻다

Track 01

옛날 황해도 황주에 심학규라는 사람이 살고 있었다. 그는 앞을 보지 못해 심 봉사라고 불렸다.

심 봉사는 행동이 바르고 곧은 마음을 지닌 사람이어서 마을 사람들은 그를 군자와 같다며 칭찬했다.

어느 날, 심 봉사가 그의 아내 곽 씨에게 말했다.

> **TIP!** Since olden times, Confucian society has called people of great learning and virtue 군자, considering them an object of respect.

"우리 집안이 양반의 후손인데 내 나이 스물에 앞을 못 보게 되고, 집안 형편마저 기울어 이렇게 부인을 고생시키니 미안하오."

심 봉사의 말을 듣고 곽 씨가 말했다.

> 마저: A postpositional particle that indicates an addition to the last thing remaining in the current state or degree of affairs.

"그런 말씀 하지 마세요. 부부는 한 몸이라고 했습니다. 하늘이 당신을 제 짝으로 보내실 때는 다 이유가 있는 것입니다. 그러니 다시는 그런 생각하지 마세요."

봉사 blind person | **곧다** upstanding (of proper and unwavering character) | **양반** nobleman | **후손** descendant | **형편이 기울다** to be in a bad situation or state | **부인** a word that a man from a noble family used to address his wife in the past

곽 씨 역시 마음씨가 곱고 기품 있는 여인이었다. 곽 씨는 앞 못
보는 남편 대신 살림을 꾸려 나가기 위해 안 해 본 일이 없었다.
그중에서 곽 씨가 가장 잘하는 일은 바로 바느질이었다.
곽 씨는 낮밤을 가리지 않고 손이 닳도록 삯바느질을 했다. 그렇게
모은 돈으로 앞 못 보는 남편을
정성스럽게 돌봤다. 심 봉사는

> 손이 닳도록: Means to use one's hands to the
> extent that they become damaged.

현명한 아내를 만난 것에 감사했고, 곽 씨도 어진 남편을 만난 것에
감사했다.

그런데 행복해 보이는 이 부부에게도 걱정이 하나 있었다. 혼인한
지 스무 해가 넘도록 자식이 없는 것이었다. 심 봉사가 아내에게
말했다.

"부인, 우리에게 자식이 없어 대가 끊어지게 되었으니 어떡하면
좋겠소?"

> 대 is a succession in a descending bloodline and
> family tree; in this phrase, because the couple
> has no children, it is said that their family line has
> been ended (대가 끊어지게 되었다).

부부는 아침마다 정화수를
떠 놓고 자식을 갖게 해 달라고
빌었다. 그리고 명산을 찾아가 부처님께 정성을 다해 기도하고
불공을 드렸다. 그러던 어느 날, 곽 씨가 지난밤에 꾼 이상한 꿈
이야기를 들려주었다.

기품 elegance | **삯바느질** sewing work done for money | **현명하다** to be wise | **어질다** to be
virtuous | **혼인하다** to marry | **정화수** freshly drawn water | **명산** famous mountain, renowned
mountain | **불공을 드리다** to offer up Buddhist prayers

"제가 꿈에서 바느질을 하고 있는데 갑자기 하늘에 오색구름이 펼쳐지고 집 안에 향기가 가득하더니 한 선녀가 학을 타고 내려왔어요. 선녀는 머리에 화관을 쓰고, 화려한 옷을 입고 있었어요. 아! 그리고 옥으로 만든 노리개에서 움직일 때마다 맑은 소리가 났어요. 그런데 그 선녀가 계수나무 가지를 들고 제 앞에 오더니 절을 하더라고요. 지금도 그 향기로운 냄새와 맑은 소리가 생생해요."

오색구름 five-colored clouds, glowing clouds | **선녀** fairy | **학** crane | **화관** wreath, crown of flowers | **옥** jade | **노리개** norigae, traditional ornament worn by Korean women | **계수나무** laurel tree

심 봉사는 아내의 이야기를 듣고 나서 말했다.

"나 역시 당신과 같은 꿈을 꾸었소. 이는 하늘이 우리에게 자식을 보내신다는 태몽이 분명하오."

심 봉사의 말대로 곽 씨는 임신하여 배가 점점 불러왔다. 곽 씨는 아이가 쓸 옷과 이불을 만들면서 건강하고 착한 아이를 낳기를 빌었다. 심 봉사도 새벽마다 절에 가서 감사 기도를 했다. 부부는 아이 생각만 하면 좋아서 입이 벌어졌다.

태몽을 꾸고 정확히 열 달이 지난 날, 곽 씨는 딸을 낳았다. 대를 이을 아들이 아니라 실망하는 곽 씨에게 심 봉사가 말했다.

"나는 부인이 순산한 것이 무엇보다 기쁘오. 우리 이 아이를 잘 길러 여생을 행복하게 보냅시다."

심 봉사는 첫국밥을 지어 삼신상에 올려놓고 아이가 무사히 잘 자라기를 기도했다.

"우리 아이가 이렇게 무사히 태어나게 해 주셔서 감사합니다. 앞으로 산모와 아이 모두 건강하게 복 많이 받고 오래오래 살 수 있도록 해 주시옵소서. 비나이다 비나이다."

> **TIP!** Samsin is the goddess who blesses people with children, also called 삼신할머니. An offering table is prepared for Samsin and prayers are made for the health of mother and child. Right after a birth, the seaweed and rice that was placed on the table for Samsin are prepared as a first meal to be fed to the mother.

> V + -(으)옵소서: An archaic expression indicating a respectful request or prayer.

태몽 conception dream (a dream foretelling the conception of a baby) | 배가 부르다 (figuratively) for a stomach to bulge because of a pregnancy | 입이 벌어지다 to be left open-mouthed (an indication of great happiness or surprise) | 순산하다 to have a safe labor | 여생 rest of one's life

그러나 곽 씨는 아이를 낳은 후 몸 상태가 점점 나빠졌다. 곽 씨가 힘겹게 말했다.

"우리 부부의 인연은 여기까지인가 봅니다. 우리 딸의 이름을 눈 맑을 '청' 자를 써서 청이라고 지어요. 앞 못 보는 당신에게 청이가 눈이 되어 준다면 제가 안심하고 떠날 수 있겠어요. 또 제가 끼던 옥가락지를 청이에게 남길 테니 훗날 저세상에서 우리 모녀가 만날 때 서로 알아볼 수 있게 해 주세요."

> 저세상: Means the world on the other side, where one goes after death; another word for the afterlife.

이 말을 마치고 곽 씨는 그만 숨을 거두었다. 청이를 낳은 지 꼭 칠 일째 되는 날이었다.

> 숨을 거두다: A more gentle way of saying "to die."
> (Syn.) 세상을 떠나다 (to leave this world),
> 눈을 감다 (to close one's eyes),
> 운명하다 (to pass away)

옥가락지 jade ring | **훗날** someday, the future

2

심청, 장님 아버지 밑에서 잘 자라다

Track 02

부인을 잃은 심 봉사는 하늘이 무너지는 것 같았다. 하지만 그의 곁에서 젖을 달라고 우는 청이가 있었기에 마냥 슬픔에 빠져 있을 수만은 없었다.

> 하늘이 무너지다: (lit. for the sky to fall down) Expresses someone receiving a large shock or facing an unexpected difficulty and being greatly discouraged.

밤새 청이를 어르던 심 봉사는 새벽닭이 우는 소리를 듣고 젖동냥을 하러 길을 나섰다. 지팡이로 앞을 더듬으며 길을 찾아가던

> 새벽닭: A rooster who crows when dawn breaks; in the time before clocks, people knew that dawn was coming when they heard the rooster crow.

심 봉사의 귀에 우물가의 두레박 소리와 아낙네들의 말소리가 들렸다. 심 봉사는 소리가 나는 곳으로 가까이 가서 말했다.

"여보시오, 부인님들. 우리 청이 젖 좀 먹여 주시오. 태어나서 칠 일 만에 어미 잃고, 앞 못 보는 아비 손에 자라서 배고파 죽을 지경이오. 댁의 아기 먹이고 남은

> A가 B의 손에 자라다: Means that B raised A.

젖이 있다면 불쌍한 우리 청이에게 한 모금만 나눠 주오."

장님 blind person | 어르다 to humor or coddle | 젖동냥 begging for breast milk | 더듬다 to fumble | 우물가 well side | 두레박 bucket | 아낙네 woman, wife | 여보시오 A word used when calling to someone close by (lit. "look over here") | 어미 mother (a less formal word than 어머니) | 아비 father (a less formal word than 아버지) | 지경 situation, state, condition | 모금 sip

한 아낙네가 심 봉사에게 말했다.

"아이, 딱해라. 마침 옆집 부인이 해산한 지 며칠 되지 않았으니 내가 부탁하여 보겠소."

"고맙소. 고맙소. 정말 고맙소."

심 봉사는 거듭 감사 인사를 했다. 잠시 후, 심 봉사는 우물가에서 만난 아낙네의 도움으로 청이에게 젖을 먹일 수 있었다. 허겁지겁 젖을 빨던 청이는 배가 부르자 울음을 멈추었다.

"에그, 어린 것이 배가 많이 고팠던 모양이네."

젖을 먹이던 부인이 심청을 안쓰럽게 보며 말했다. 이날부터 심 봉사는 본격적으로 청이에게 먹일 젖을 얻으러 다녔는데 처음이 어렵지 점점 도가

> 도가 트다: Expresses becoming proficient in something and knowing how to do it well.

텄다. 동네 부인들도 심 봉사와 심청 부녀를 딱하게 여겨 살 방도를 함께 궁리해 주었다. 여러 사람의 도움으로 심청은 배부르게 먹으며 자랄 수 있었다.

심청이 조금 더 크자, 심 봉사는 청이를 재워 두고 이 집 저 집으로 쌀을 구걸하러 다녔다. 그 쌀로 청이에게 죽도 끓여 주고 청이가 좋아하는 엿도 사 먹일 수 있었다. 심 봉사의 사랑 속에 심청은 쑥쑥 자라 어느덧 일곱 살이 되었다. 심청이 심 봉사에게 말했다.

딱하다 to be pitiful, to be pitiable | 해산하다 to deliver a child | 거듭 again, repeatedly | 허겁지겁 hurriedly, hastily | 에그 a sound made when seeing something unfortunate or pitiful | 안쓰럽다 to be pitiful, to be pitiable | 본격적 regular | 방도 way, means | 궁리하다 to deliberate, to think about | 구걸하다 to beg | 엿 starch syrup candy, hard taffy

"아버지, 말 못하는 까마귀도 날 힘이 생기면 먹이를 물어와 부모님을 섬긴다고 합니다. 아버지 덕으로 이만큼 컸으니 이제 먹을 걸 구하는 일은 제게 맡겨 주세요."

심청의 말을 듣고 심 봉사가 말했다.

"우리 청이, 기특하구나. 하지만 너를 위해 밥을 얻으러 다니는 일은 고생이 아니라

> V/A + -(는)구나: Draws attention to new information that the speaker has learned. Often used with a meaning of admiration and also when speaking to oneself.

행복이고 보람이니

네 부탁은 들어주기 어렵겠구나."

"앞 못 보는 아버지께서 밥을 얻으러 가다 넘어져 병이라도 나시면 그 불효를 어찌 감당하겠습니까? 제 부탁을 들어주세요."

심청의 계속되는 부탁에 심 봉사는 마지못해 허락했고 심청은 아버지를 대신해 밥을 얻으러 다니기 시작했다. 겨울바람이 해진 저고리와 치마를 뚫고 들어왔다. 심청의 가녀린 몸은 사정없이 떨렸고, 짚신이 다 떨어져 드러난 버선 없는 맨발은 꽁꽁 얼었다.

하지만 심청은 아버지를 도울 수 있다는 생각으로 밥 짓는 냄새가 나는 부엌에 들어가 말했다.

"혹여 남는 밥을 한 숟가락 나눠 주신다면 추운 날 찬 방에서 기다리시는 부친께서 허기를 면할 수 있겠나이다."

> V + -나이다: Primarily an old form of speech used to describe a fact very politely.

까마귀 crow | 섬기다 to serve, to take care of | 기특하다 to be admirable | 불효 filial impiety, disobedience to one's parents | 어찌 how, what | 감당하다 to manage, to handle | 마지못하다 to be forced to, to do something reluctantly | 해지다 to wear down, to fray | 가녀리다 to be slender | 사정없이 mercilessly, severely

"에그, 딱해. 밥을 좀 줄 테니 가져가거라."

심청의 모습을 보는 사람마다 어린

심청의 효심에 감탄하며 아낌없이

> V + -거라: Expresses a command (has a more old-fashioned feeling then -아/어라).

먹을 것을 주었다. 이 집 저 집에서 내어 준 나물에 쌀밥, 콩밥,

수수밥이 뒤섞여 형형색색이었다. 이렇게 심 봉사의 밥상에 매일

오곡밥이 올랐다.

"아버지, 따뜻한 물을 국 삼아 천천히 드세요."

심청은 아버지의 손에 수저를 쥐어 주고 반찬도 올려 주며

심 봉사를 극진히 봉양했다.

효심 filial devotion, affection for one's parents | 감탄하다 to admire | 수수 sorghum | 뒤섞이다
to be mixed | 형형색색 variety | 오곡밥 five-grain rice | 극진히 devotedly, kindly, with all one's
heart | 봉양하다 to serve / support one's parents

고생하는 심청을 보며 심 봉사는 마음이 아팠지만 심청은
자식으로서 당연히 해야 할 일이라며 오히려 심 봉사를 위로했다.
그리고 열세 살이 되었을 때부터 삯바느질을 시작해 밤낮으로
열심히 일했다. 다행히 어머니 곽 씨를 닮아 심청은 바느질 솜씨가
무척 뛰어났다. 부지런하고 알뜰한 심청의 노력 덕분에 심청이
열다섯이 되었을 때부터는 밥을 얻어 오지 않아도 부녀가 충분히
끼니를 해결할 수 있었다.

알뜰하다 to be thrifty, to be frugal ｜ **끼니** meal

3

심 봉사, 공양미 300석을 약속하다

Track 03

마을 사람들은 심청의 효심을 입이 닳도록 칭찬했다. 게다가
심청은 뛰어난 일솜씨에 빼어난 미모까지
갖추고 있었기에 심청에 대한 이야기는

> 입이 닳도록: Means that people complimented them to the point that their mouths wore down.

입소문을 타고 이웃 마을 무릉촌에까지 퍼졌다. 무릉촌에 사는 장
승상 부인은 소문을 듣고 심청을 몹시 만나고 싶어 했다. 부인은
일찍이 남편 장 승상을 여의고,

> 승상 (prime minister) is the name of a government post, and "Prime Minister Jang" means a prime minister who has the family name of Jang.

아들 삼 형제는 모두 한양에서
벼슬살이를 하고 있어 홀로 지내고 있던 터였다.

승상 부인은 심청의 집에 사람을 보내 만나고 싶다는 뜻을 전했다.
소식을 전달받은 심청은 심 봉사에게 말했다.

"아버지, 승상 댁 부인께서 오라고 하시니 잠시 다녀오겠습니다.
진지는 차려 두었으니 제가 늦거든 아버지 먼저 잡수세요."

심 봉사가 당부했다.

"그래, 조심해서 다녀오고 승상 댁 부인을 만나거든 예의범절에
어긋나지 않게 행동해야 한다."

빼어나다 to be remarkable, to be exceptional | **미모** good looks, beauty | **여의다** to lose someone, to be bereaved | **벼슬살이** living as a government official | **터** circumstances | **진지** meal (polite speech) | **당부하다** to request | **예의범절** etiquette, good manners

"네, 그럴게요."

심청은 아버지를 혼자 두고 오랜 시간 집을 비우는 일이 마음에
걸렸지만 별일 없을 거라고 자신을 달랬다. 심청이 승상 댁에
도착하니 하인이 나와 심청을 집 안으로 데리고 들어갔다. 심청은
대궐 같은 집을 보고 눈이 휘둥그레졌다. 큰 나무들이 집을 둘러쌌고
마당에는 화사한 꽃이 만발했으며 넓은 연못에는 금붕어가 한가롭게
놀고 있으니, 집의 규모와 화려함이 비길 데가 없었다.

승상 부인은 심청이 왔다는 얘기를
들고 버선발로 뛰어나와 반겼다.

> 비길 데 없다: Means nothing to compare ⒮ⓨⓝ 비할 데 없다, 견줄 데 없다

"네가 도화동에 사는 심청이냐?
어서 오너라. 듣던 대로 빼어난
처녀로구나."

> 버선발로 뛰어나오다: (lit. to run out in stockinged feet) 버선발 means feet that are only wearing socks, so this idiom means to anticipate something to the degree that one will run out without even putting on one's shoes.

승상 부인과 심청은 수도 놓고, 다과도

> N + (이)냐: A very informal sentence ending that expresses a question

먹으며 이런저런 이야기를 나누었다. 승상 부인은 심청의
예의 바른 말과 행동이 마음에 쏙 들어 심청이 딸처럼 여겨졌다.
부인이 말했다.

"심청아, 승상이 일찍 세상을 떠나시고 자식들도 멀리 있으니 내
곁에는 말벗이 없구나. 네가 수양딸로 들어오면 글공부도 시켜 주고
친딸처럼 길러서 좋은 곳에 시집도 보내 줄 수 있는데, 너의 생각은
어떠하냐?"

마음에 걸리다 to weigh on one's mind | **대궐** palace | **휘둥그레지다** to become wide-eyed |
화사하다 to be beautiful, to be gorgeous | **만발하다** to be in full bloom | **금붕어** goldfish | **한가롭다**
leisurely, to be unhurried | **수를 놓다** to embroider | **다과** refreshments | **쏙** very much | **말벗**
companion to talk to | **수양딸** adopted daughter

뜻밖의 말에 심청은 당황했지만, 예의를 갖춰 말했다.

"미천한 저를 그렇게 생각해 주시니 감사합니다. 그러나 제 한 몸 편하기 위해 부인의 말씀을 따른다면 앞 못 보는 제 아버지는 누가 돌보겠습니까? 저는 아버지의 눈이 되어 평생 곁에서 모시고자 합니다. 부인께서는 제 뜻을 헤아려 주시고 서운하게 생각하지 말아 주세요."

승상 부인은 심청의 말에 감탄하며 말했다.

"과연 효녀로구나. 내가 생각이 짧아 과한 부탁을 했으니 섭섭하게 생각하지 말아 주렴.

> V + -(으)렴 : Makes the speaker's words soft and familiar, and expresses a command or request in a roundabout way.

즐겁게 담소를 나눈 후 심청이 돌아갈 때가 되자, 승상 부인은 심청에게 양식과 옷감을 싸 주었다.

"내 마음이니 사양하지 말고 가지고 가거라. 다음에도 와서 내 말벗이 되어 주렴."

심청은 자신을 딸처럼 생각해 주는 승상 부인이 정말 고마웠다. 심청은 꼭 그러하겠다고 말하고 부인이 준 양식과 옷감을 가지고 집으로 향했다.

미천하다 humble, lowly | 과하다 to be too much, to be excessive | 담소 friendly chat | 양식 food, provisions | 옷감 cloth, fabric | 사양하다 to turn down, to refuse

그때 심 봉사는 점심때가 훌쩍 지났지만, 밥 먹을 생각도 하지
않고 심청을 기다렸다. 방 안에서 기다리던 심 봉사는 바람 부는
소리에 심청이 왔나 싶어 마당으로 나와서 또 한참을 기다렸다.
그러다 행인이 지나가는 소리에 또 심청이 왔나 싶어 대문 밖으로
나왔다. 그렇게 한 걸음 한 걸음 걷다 보니 심 봉사는 개천에
이르렀고, 발을 헛디뎌 그만 물에 풍덩 빠져 버렸다.

심 봉사가 소리쳤다.

"사람 살려! 거기 아무도 없소? 어푸어푸, 이게 웬 날벼락이냐!
아이고 나 죽겠네! 사람 살려!"

훌쩍 great amount | 행인 passerby | 개천 small stream | 헛디디다 to slip, to lose one's footing |
풍덩 splash | 어푸어푸 a painful sound made when one has fallen into water and drinks it in (or
describes this sight) | 날벼락 something unexpected

그때 마침 몽은사 승려가 절을 새로 짓기 위해 시주 장부를 들고 마을로 내려왔다가 어디에선가 살려 달라는 소리를 들었다. 소리가 나는 쪽으로 달려간 승려는 개천에 빠진 심 봉사를 발견해서 물 밖으로 끌어내었다. 심 봉사는 힘겹게 숨을 내쉬며 말했다.

"누구신지 모르겠지만 죽을 뻔한 목숨을 살려 주니 정말 고맙소."

승려가 심 봉사에게 답했다.

"몽은사 승려요."

심 봉사는 죽을 뻔한 자신을 살려 준 것이 부처님의 은혜라고 생각했다. 승려는 앞을 보지 못하는 심 봉사를 위해 집까지 업어다 주고는 물었다.

"앞도 못 보는 분이 어쩌다 물에 빠지게 되었소?"

심 봉사는 지금까지의 일을 승려에게 말했다. 전후 사정을 알게 된 승려는 혀를 차며 말했다.

"나무아미타불. 당신이 지금 눈이 먼 것은 전생에 지은 죄 때문이오. 부처님께 공양미 삼백 석을 올리고 정성을 다해 불공을 드린다면 눈을 뜰 수 있소."

> 나무아미타불: Means "with the will to return to Amitabha;" it is said that if you memorize this phrase, you can achieve the things you want or receive salvation.

몽은사 Mongeunsa Temple | 승려 Buddhist monk | 시주 donation, offering | 장부 ledger | 끌어내다 to drag someone out | 내쉬다 to exhale, to breath out | 혀를 차다 to cluck one's tongue | 전생 previous life | 공양미 rice offered to the Buddha

심 봉사는 눈을 뜰 수 있다는 말에 놀라서 집안 사정은 생각하지 않고 다급하게 말했다.

"그게 정말이오? 그럼 삼백 석을 올리겠소."

승려는 기막히다는 듯이 말했다.

"쯧쯧, 집을 둘러보니 가난하기

이를 데 없는데 쌀 삼백 석을 무슨 수로 마련한다는 말이오?"

승려의 걱정에도 심 봉사는 아랑곳하지 않고 말했다.

"부처님께 거짓 약속은 하지 않을 테니 어서 '심학규 쌀 삼백 석'이라고 시주 장부에 적어 내 눈을 뜨게 해 주십시오."

심 봉사의 거듭된 요청에 승려는 장부에 심학규의 이름을 적고 돌아갔다.

> 석: An old unit of measurement, also called 섬, equivalent to about 100kg of rice.

다급하게 urgently, hurriedly | **기막히다** to be amazing | **이를 데 없다** unspeakably, as ... as can be |
수 means, way | **마련하다** to prepare, to arrange | **아랑곳하지 않다** without concern or consideration |
거듭되다 to repeat

4

심청, 공양미 300석에 몸을 팔다

Track 04

승려가 돌아간 뒤 심 봉사는 아무도 없는 방에 가만히 앉아 생각에 잠겼다. 대책 없이 공양미 삼백 석을 약속한 자신의 성급한 행동이 생각할수록 어이없고 후회가 되었다. 복을 얻으려다 오히려 죄를 짓게 생겼으니 이 일을 어떻게 해야 할지 막막했다.

이때 심청이 집에 돌아와 물에 젖은 심 봉사의 모습을 보고 놀라 물었다.

"어머나! 아버지, 저를 찾아다니시다가 물에 빠지셨나요?"

심 봉사는 고민에 빠져 아무 소리도 듣지 못했다.

"에그, 우리 아버지 많이 추우신가 보네. 말씀도 안 하시고. 진지는 드셨어요?"

심청이 밥상을 살펴보니 차려 둔 음식이 그대로 있었다. 심청은 아버지가 밥도 제대로 못 드시고 혼자 딸을 기다리다 변을 당했다고 생각하니 가슴이 찢어질 듯했다.

> 가슴이 찢어질 듯하다: A phrase expressing a sadness so large that it feels painful, as if one's heart were being torn apart.

성급하다 to be hasty, to be rash | 어이없다 to be dumbfounded | 막막하다 to be forlorn, to be at a loss | 변을 당하다 to have an accident

'눈먼 우리 아버지를 집에 두고 나 혼자 승상 댁에서 잘 놀고 잘 먹었으니 이게 죄가 아니고 무엇이냐.'

심청이 흐르는 눈물을 감추며 심 봉사에게 말했다.

"우리 아버지, 많이 시장하시겠네. 여기 새 옷이 있으니 갈아입고 계세요. 다시 따뜻한 진지 지어 올릴게요."

심 봉사는 더듬더듬 옷을 집어 입었다. 심청은 서둘러 부엌으로 가서 승상 댁에서 가져온 양식으로 저녁을 지어 왔다.

"아버지, 진지 드세요."

그런데 맛있는 반찬 냄새가 코를 찔러도, 청이가 손에 수저를 쥐어 줘도 심 봉사는 도저히 밥을 먹을 수가 없었다. 심청이 걱정스럽게 물었다.

> 냄새가 코를 찌르다: (lit. for a smell to pierce one's nose) Means for a scent to strongly stimulate one's sense of smell.

"아버지, 어디 편찮으세요?"

"아니다."

"그럼, 제가 늦게 돌아와 화나셨나요?"

"아니다."

"그럼 무슨 근심이라도 있으신가요?"

심 봉사는 계속되는 심청의 질문에 마지못해 내막을 털어놓았다. 이야기를 다 들은 심청은 아버지를 안심시켰다.

"아버지, 걱정 마세요. 부처님 앞에 약속하고 후회하면 효험이 없어요. 아버지가 눈을 뜨실 수 있다면 어떻게든 공양미 삼백 석을 마련해 몽은사에 보낼게요."

시장하다 to be hungry | **더듬더듬** falteringly | **내막** inside story | **털어놓다** to reveal, to confess | **효험** effectiveness, efficacy

"하지만 우리 형편에 공양미 삼백 석을 어찌
마련할 수 있겠느냐? 눈을 뜰 수 있다는 말에
경거망동했으니 이 일을 어찌하면 좋단 말이냐?"

경거망동(輕擧妄動)하다:
Means for a person to
act thoughtlessly and
without caution.

심 봉사가 가슴을 치며 후회했다. 하지만 심청은 오히려 아버지를
위로했다.

"아버지, 지성이면 감천이니 방법이 있을 것입니다."

그리고 심청은 그날부터 정화수를
떠 놓고 간절히 빌기 시작했다.

지성(至誠)이면 감천(感天)이다: Means that if
one's devotion is extreme, even heaven
will be moved; a saying meaning that no
matter what, even difficult things can be
achieved if one puts one's heart into it.

"신이시여, 앞 못 보는 제 아비가
온갖 고생 다 하며 저를 키웠으니, 이제 이 한 몸 바쳐서라도 아비가
눈을 뜰 수 있다면 소원이 없겠나이다. 부디 공양미 삼백 석을 구할
길을 열어 주시어 아비의 눈을 뜨게 해 주옵소서."

이렇게 정성껏 빌던 어느 날 한 무리의 장사꾼들이 열다섯 살
처녀를 산다는 소문이 마을 전체에 빠르게

N + 껏: Means "all of" something

퍼졌다. 이웃집 할머니가 심청의 집을 지나가면서 혼잣말을 했다.

"세상 참 별일이 다 있네. 내가 지금까지 살면서 사람을 사겠다는
그런 해괴한 말은 처음 들어 보는군. 그것도 열다섯 살 먹은 처녀를!
쯧쯧."

무리 group, band | 장사꾼 merchant, trader | 혼잣말 talking to oneself | 해괴하다 to be strange,
to be outrageous

마침 마당에서 기도를 드리던 심청은 귀가 번쩍 뜨였다. 심청이
밖으로 나가 할머니에게 물었다.

> 귀가 번쩍 뜨이다: (lit. for ears to open wide) Means that a certain word or speech is so convincing that one is drawn in without hesitation.

"할머니, 그게 무슨 말이에요? 처녀를
산다고요?"

"아이고, 심청아. 그래. 열다섯 살 먹은 처녀라면 돈을 얼마든지
주고 사겠다는 말을 내가 두 귀로 똑똑히 들었다. 세상이 어떻게
돌아가는지!"

"할머니, 그 장사꾼들 지금 어디에 있는지 아세요?"

"나루터에 그 사람들 배가 있다고 하더구나. 관아에 가서 그
사람들 좀 잡아가라고 해라."

> V + -더구나: Reports new information learned from a past experience, or expresses feelings being recollected. A meaning of awe can also be used together with this.

심청은 할머니에게 인사를 하고
허겁지겁 나루터로 향했다. 나루터에는
장사꾼들이 모여 있었다. 심청이 장사꾼들에게 가까이 다가가
물었다.

"그대들은 왜 젊은 처녀를 사려고 하시오?"

"우리는 중국 남경에 가서 장사하는 뱃사람들인데, 배가 인당수를
지날 때면 위험하기 짝이 없소. 그런데 소문에 젊은 처녀를 제물로
바치면 험난한 뱃길이 무사히 열리고
장사도 잘 되어 큰 이익을 낼 수
있다고 하기에 값을 묻지 않고 처녀를 사려는 것이오."

> A + -기 짝이 없다: Means that something is so incredible or as severe that there is nothing to which it can be compared.

나루터 dock | **관아** government office | **뱃사람** sailor | **인당수** the Indangsu Sea | **제물** sacrificial
offering | **험난하다** to be dangerous | **이익을 내다** to make a profit

'하늘이 나를 돕는구나!'

그 말을 듣고 심청은 하늘이 자신의 기도를 들어줬다고 생각했다.

"나는 십오 세 심청이라고 하오. 공양미 삼백 석을 부처님께
올리면 앞 못 보는 아비가 눈을 뜰 수 있다는데, 집안이 가난하여
장만할 수 없었소. 공양미 삼백 석을 준다면 내 몸을 제물로 팔겠소."

장사꾼 무리의 우두머리가 말했다.

"효심이 아름답구려. 낭자의 처지는 딱하지만 우리에게는 좋은
기회이니 즉시 원하는 값을
치르겠소. 배는 다음 달 보름에 떠나오."

> 낭자: A polite, archaic term for an unmarried woman.

장만하다 to prepare, to procure | 우두머리 chief, leader

5

심청, 인당수에 몸을 던지다

Track 05

'다음 달 보름이면 아버지 곁을 떠나야 하는구나.'

심청은 이별을 생각하면 슬프다가도 아버지가 눈 뜰 생각을 하면
힘이 났다.

"아버지, 공양미 삼백 석을 몽은사에 보냈어요. 그러니 이제
근심하지 마세요."

심 봉사가 눈을 동그랗게 떴다.

"뭐? 네가 그 많은 쌀을 어떻게 마련했느냐?"

심청은 거짓말로 심 봉사를 안심시켰다.

"지난번 장 승상 댁 부인께서 저를 수양딸로 삼고 싶다 하시기에
거절하고 돌아왔습니다."

"그래? 그런 일이 있었느냐? 그런데 그 일이 공양미 삼백 석과
무슨 상관이냐?"

"아버지 눈을 뜨게 해 드리고 싶은데 공양미 삼백 석을 마련할
길은 없어 승상 부인께 말씀드렸더니 선뜻 공양미 삼백 석을
내주셨습니다."

선뜻 gladly, willingly

"아니, 이렇게 감사한 일이!"

"네, 그래서 그 은혜를 갚기 위해 승상 부인께 수양딸이 되겠다고
했어요."

심 봉사는 자신 때문에 심청이 남의 집 딸이 된다고 생각하니
미안하기도 하고 서운하기도 했다.

"내가 눈을 얻고 딸을 잃는구나."

하지만 곧 생각이 달라졌다.

"아니야, 오히려 잘되었다. 여태 어미 없이 고생만 한 우리 청이,
부잣집에 들어가 편하게 살 수 있다면 이보다 좋은 일이 어디
있겠느냐? 청아, 승상 댁에서 너를 언제 데리고 간다고 하시더냐?"

"다음 달 보름에요."

> V/A + –더냐: Expresses a request to someone to recall a fact they experienced in the past. Often used colloquially.

"아, 얼마 남지 않았구나.
그래도 괜찮다. 너만 잘 산다면 난 혼자 살아도 괜찮아. 괜찮고말고.
딸 덕에 내가 환한 세상 보겠네. 이제 봉사 소리 안 듣고 살겠구나."

심 봉사는 심청의 속도 모르고 신이 났다. 그런 심 봉사의 모습을
보는 심청의 마음은 기쁨과 슬픔이 한데 뒤섞였다.

심청은 그날부터 죽을 준비를 차근차근했다. 아버지가 철따라
입을 옷을 꿰매 옷장에 넣어 두고, 버선도 만들어 쌓아 두었다. 갓과
망건도 새 것으로 장만해 걸어 두어 심 봉사가 불편함이 없도록
하였다.

여태 so far, still | **한데** together, at one time | **차근차근** step by step, methodically | **꿰매다** to sew | **갓** gat, a traditional hat worn by men during the Joseon dynasty | **망건** manggeon, a headband used to keep hair in place before wearing a gat

시간은 쏜살같이 지나가 약속한 날이 벌써 하루 앞으로 다가왔다. 심청은 잠을 이룰 수가 없었다. 앞 못 보는 아버지가 눈을 뜨는 것만큼 좋은 일도 없었지만 심청이 죽고 나면 아버지 혼자 어찌 사실까 걱정도 되었다. 그리고 아버지를 위해 스스로 제물이 되겠다고 했지만 죽음이 두렵지 않은 것은 아니었다. 심청은 밤새 한숨도 못 자고 닭 우는 소리를 들으며 해가 뜨는 모습을 지켜봤다.

약속한 보름날 아침이 되었다. 심청은 깨끗한 옷으로 갈아입고 어머니가 남긴 옥가락지를 꼈다. 그리고 아버지께 마지막 밥상을 차려 드리려고 문을 열고 부엌으로 갔다. 집 밖에는 벌써 뱃사람들이 찾아와 기다리고 있었다. 심청이 뱃사람들에게 말했다.

"오늘 배가 떠나는 날이지요. 아버님께 마지막 진지를 지어 올릴 시간을 주세요."

"네, 그러지요. 하지만 너무 늦으면 안 됩니다."

심청은 정성껏 밥을 지어 아버지 앞으로 가져갔다. 아버지와 밥상을 마주한 심청은 아버지 수저 위에 반찬을 올려 드리며 소리 죽여 흐르는 눈물을 닦았다.

> 소리를 죽이다: (lit. to kill a sound) "죽이다 (to kill)" here means to reduce or stop the sound of footsteps, breathing, etc., so this means to suppress a sound so that it will not be heard.

심 봉사가 말했다.

"청아, 오늘 반찬이 왜 이리 좋으냐? 마치 생일날 같구나. 어느 집 결혼식이 있었느냐? 어느 집 제사가 있었느냐?"

쏜살같이 swiftly, like an arrow | **보름날** the day of the full moon (the 15th day of a month of the Korean lunar calendar)

그러다 무릎을 탁 치며 말했다.

"참, 오늘이 바로 보름날이로구나. 승상 댁에서 너를 데리러 오는 날을 그만 깜박 잊고 있었구나. 간밤에 네가 큰 수레를 타고 가는 꿈을 꾸었는데 아마도 승상 댁에서 너에게 가마를 보내실 모양이다."

그 꿈은 분명 심청이 죽을 꿈이었다. 이 말을 들은 심청이 더는 아비를 속일 수 없어 심 봉사의 목을 끌어안고 통곡하며 말했다.

"아이고, 아버지! 제가 아버지를 속였어요. 누가 공양미 삼백 석을 그냥 주겠어요. 인당수에 바칠 제물로 뱃사람들에게 제 몸을 팔았으니 바로 오늘이 제가 떠나는 날입니다. 밖에 뱃사람들이 저를 기다리고 있어요. 아버지 절 받으세요. 저는 이제 가야 합니다."

심 봉사는 하늘이 무너지는 것 같았다.

"그게 무슨 소리냐? 딸을 죽여 자기 눈을 뜨는 몹쓸 아비가 세상에 어디 있단 말이냐? 너 없이 눈을 뜨는 일이 무슨 의미가 있겠느냐? 청아, 가지 마라. 제발 가지 마라."

그리고 문을 열어 밖에서 기다리고 있는 뱃사람들에게 고함을 쳤다.

"이놈들아! 산 사람을 제물로 바치는 일이 세상 어디에 있단 말이냐? 너희가 그러고도 사람이냐? 어미 없이 눈먼 아비 보살피느라 고생만 한 우리 청이를 누가 데려간단 말이냐? 쌀도 필요 없고, 눈 뜨는 것도 싫다. 지금 당장 이곳을 떠나라!"

간밤 last night, the previous evening | **수레** wagon | **가마** palanquin | **통곡하다** to wail |
몹쓸 wicked, evil | **고함을 치다** to shout

심청이 아버지를 말리며 말했다.

"아버지, 공양미 삼백 석에 몸을 팔기로 약속한 사람은 저예요. 저 사람들 탓이 아니에요. 제가 바라는 것은 아버지가 눈 뜨시고 건강하게 사시는 것뿐이에요. 부디 빨리 눈을 뜨시고 평안히 사세요."

말을 마친 심청은 심 봉사에게 절을 올렸다. 그리고 뱃사람들을 향해 떨어지지 않는 발걸음으로 집을 나섰다. 심 봉사가 마당으로 뛰어나오며 울부짖었다.

"안 된다. 안 된다. 나만 두고 어딜 가느냐? 청아! 제발 부탁이니 그냥 돌아오너라. 제발 아비한테 오너라. 이 아비가 어리석어 공양미 삼백 석을 약속했으니 그 벌은 내가 받으마. 청아!"

심청은 뒤를 돌아보며 심 봉사에게 인사했다.

"아버지, 부디 건강하세요."

뱃사람들이 그 모습을 보고 안타까운 마음에 말했다.

"심 낭자의 효심을 봐서 심 봉사가 앞으로도 굶지 않고 잘 살 수 있도록 우리가 좀 도와주면 어떻겠소?"

"그게 좋겠소."

뱃사람들은 심 봉사의 집에 돈과 곡식, 옷감을 부족함 없이 가져왔다. 심 봉사와 심청에 대한 소문은 금방 마을 전체에 알려졌다.

평안히 in peace | **울부짖다** to wail, to howl

뱃사람들이 이제 심청을 데려가려고 했을 때 승상 부인이 뒤늦게 이 소식을 듣고 하녀를 시켜 심청을 불렀다. 하녀를 따라가니 문밖에서 승상 부인이 심청을 발견하고 말했다.

"심청아, 네 효심이야 알겠다만, 아버지가 눈을 뜨는 것이 네가 살아 있는 것만 하겠느냐? 나는 너를 딸처럼 생각했는데 왜 진작 나와 의논해 주지 않았느냐? 내가 대신 쌀 삼백 석을 내줄 테니 뱃사람들에게 돌려주거라."

승상 부인의 말을 듣고 심청이 답했다.

"부모를 위해 정성을 다하는 것인데 어찌 이유 없는 재물을 바라겠습니까? 또한 쌀 삼백 석을 도로 돌려주면 뱃사람들의 일도 그르치게 됩니다. 부인의 하늘 같은 은혜는 제가 저승에 가서도 꼭 갚겠습니다."

말을 끝내고 눈물을 짓는 심청의 얼굴이 엄숙해서 승상 부인은 차마 더 이상 권하지 못했다. 심청은 눈물을 닦으며 승상 부인에게 말했다.

"부인을 제 전생의 부모로 알겠습니다."

부인과 그렇게 이별하고 돌아와 심청이 이별을 전하자 심 봉사는 팔을 뻗어 허우적거리며 심청을 따라가려다 그만 돌부리에 발이 걸려 넘어졌다.

"뱃사람들! 나를 데려가오. 제발 내 딸 대신 나를 데려가오!"

하녀 maid | 진작 beforehand | 재물 wealth, property | 그르치다 to ruin, to spoil | 저승 afterlife |
허우적거리다 to flail | 돌부리 stone

심청의 발소리가 멀어져 가는 소리가 들리자 심 봉사는 땅에
주저앉아 울며 소리쳤다. 하지만 아무런 대답도 돌아오지 않았다.
심 봉사는 엎드려 얼굴을 땅에 묻고 흐느꼈다.

"그럼 나도 데려가시오. 딸 없이 나 혼자 살아 뭐 하겠소. 제발
나도 함께 데려가 주오."

이 모습을 지켜보던 마을 사람들도 눈물을 흘렸다. 그러다 몇몇은
심 봉사를 달래 집으로 데려갔다. 몇몇이 심청을 배웅하기 위해 배를
타는 곳까지 따라갔다.

"혼자 된 우리 아버지 잘 부탁드려요. 그동안 도와주신 은혜를 다
갚지 못하고 떠나 죄송합니다."

심청은 자신을 따라온 마을 사람들에게 이렇게 말하고 배에
올랐다. 아무 말 못 하고 눈물만 흘리는 마을 사람들을 뒤로 한 채
심청을 태운 배는 마을을 떠났다. 심청은 배 안에서 멍하니 앉아
바다를 바라보며 두 볼에 흐르는 눈물을 닦아 냈다.

어느덧 출항한 지 닷새째가 되었다. 심청이 탄 배가 드디어
인당수를 지날 무렵, 맑던 하늘이 갑자기 어두워지더니 굵은
빗줄기가 쏟아졌다. 광풍이 불고 세차게 파도가 이는 모습이 마치
용이 일어나 꿈틀대는 듯하였다. 그러자 거친 파도에 이리저리
흔들리는 배 위에서 북소리가 울려 퍼졌다.

흐느끼다 to weep, to sob | 멍하니 blankly, absent-mindedly | 닦아 내다 to wipe, to blot | **출항하다**
to leave port, to depart | 빗줄기 streaks of rain | **광풍** gale | 세차다 to be violent | **파도가 일다**
for waves to rise up | **꿈틀대다** to wriggle, to writhe

"둥 둥 둥"

뱃사람들이 고사를 지내기 위해 북을 치는 소리였다. 그들은
고사상 앞에 모여 빌기 시작했다.

> 고사상: A table used to put out offerings of food to serve to the gods for a ritual.

"용왕님! 인당수에서 용왕님께
제물을 바치니 부디 기쁘게 받아 주시고 험한 뱃길을 안전하게
지나갈 수 있게 해 주시옵소서."

장사꾼 무리의 우두머리가 심청을 불러 말했다.

"심 낭자, 여기가 인당수요. 이제 때가 되었으니 준비하시오."

심청은 비틀거리며 배 앞쪽으로 향했다. 뱃머리에 올라서서 두
손을 모으고 이렇게 빌었다.

"하느님, 이 몸이 죽는 건 서럽지 않으니 앞 못 보는 아버지가 눈을
떠 광명을 보게 해 주시옵소서."

그리고 아버지를 떠올리며 말했다.

"아버지, 부디 만수무강하세요."

> 만수무강(萬壽無疆)하다: Means "to live a very long and safe life," usually used to greet elderly people as 만수무강하시길 기원합니다.

말을 마친 심청은 바로 물속으로
뛰어들 생각이었으나 거친 파도를
바라보니 용기가 나지 않았다. 기절할 것 같아 한참을 망설였지만
어쩔 수 없었다. 결국 심청은 무서운 마음에 두 손으로 눈을 꼭
가리고 검푸른 물속으로 뛰어들었다.

용왕님 the Dragon King, a deity of the rivers and seas | **뱃머리** bow of a boat | **광명** bright light |
기절하다 to faint, to collapse | **검푸르다** to be dark blue | **잠잠하다** to be calm, to be quiet

'아버지, 저는 이렇게 죽습니다.'

심청을 제물로 바치자 파도가 순식간에 잠잠해졌다. 고요한
인당수 위로 맑은 하늘이 펼쳐져 있었다.

6

옥황상제, 효녀 심청을 살리다

Track 06

하늘에서 모든 일을 지켜보고 있던 옥황상제가 용왕에게 명을
내렸다.

> 옥황상제: The central and greatest god of the Taoist gods. As the ruler of the heavens, he handles the destinies of all living things.

"오늘 하늘이 내린 효녀 심청이
인당수에 빠질 것이니 몸에 물 한
방울 묻지 않게 고이 모셨다가 삼 년 후 인간 세상에 돌려보내도록
하여라. 이를 조금이라도 어긴다면 용왕에게 죄를 물으리라."

이에 용왕은 모든 신하들에게
심청을 극진히 대접하라고 명했다.

> V + -(으)리라: Expresses will behind a certain action.

용궁의 모든 신하들이 모여 심청이 도착하기를 기다렸다. 그때
떨어지는 꽃잎처럼 심청의 몸이 물속으로 내려왔다. 용왕은 심청을
용궁에 모시라고 명했다.

잠시 후, 심청이 눈을 떴다. 심청은 인당수에 빠지면서 이제 죽은
목숨이라 생각했는데 눈을 뜨니 멀쩡히 살아서 아름다운 바닷속
궁궐에 있다는 것이 황당했다. 심청은 이 모든 게 꿈이 아니라는
것을 믿게 되기까지 한참의 시간이 걸렸다.

명을 내리다 to give an order | **고이** gently, with care | **용궁** the Dragon Palace, the undersea home of the Dragon King | **궁궐** palace | **황당하다** to be absurd, to be nonsensical

정신을 차린 심청이 말했다.

"제가 어찌 이런 귀한 대접을 받을 수 있단 말입니까?"

용궁의 시녀들이 답했다.

"옥황상제의 명이니 사양하지 마시고 마음 편히 지내세요."

시녀들에게 전후 상황을 들었지만 심청은 태어나서 한 번도 구경해 본 적 없는 귀한 음식을 먹고 시녀들의 시중까지 받게 되니 어리둥절하기만 했다. 용왕은 심청이 용궁에서 지내는 데 불편한 점은 없는지 아침저녁으로 살폈다.

그렇게 심청은 용궁에서 편안한 시간을 보내게 되었지만 한편으로는 혼자 계실 아버지 생각만 하면 마음이 무거웠다.

'아버지는 눈을 뜨셨을까? 내가 죽은 줄로만 알고 계실 텐데……. 아버지를 자식 먼저 떠나보내는 슬픔에 빠뜨리고 나는 호의호식하고 있으니 이런 불효가 세상에 어디 있을까.'

> 호의호식(好衣好食): (lit. "to wear fine clothes and eat fine food") Means "to be high on the hog". This indicates a life of affluence, wanting for nothing.

그러던 어느 날 시녀가 심청에게 옥진 부인이 찾아왔다고 전했다.

"옥진 부인이요?"

심청은 자신을 찾아온 이가 누구인지 궁금해하며 손님을 맞이하기 위해 자리에서 일어났다. 그때 문이 열리고 옥진 부인이 들어왔다. 옥진 부인은 천천히 심청에게 다가가 두 손으로 심청의 손을 잡았다. 그리고 참았던 눈물을 터트리며 심청의 이름을 불렀다.

시중 waiting on, serving | 어리둥절하다 to be bewildered | 터트리다 to burst into

"청아! 청아!"

옥진 부인은 바로 죽은 심청의 어미 곽 씨였다. 곽 씨는 하늘나라 광한전에 사는 신선이 되었다가 심청이 용궁에 있다는 말을 듣고 옥황상제께 허락을 받아 온 것이었다. 심청은 처음에는

> **TIP!** 광한전(Gwanghanjeon Palace or the Lunar Palace) is the name of a palace found on the moon, and Lady Okjin is the name of a female immortal who lives in 선계, a sort of fairy land.

영문을 몰라 어리둥절했지만 옥진 부인이 자신의 어머니라는 것을 알고 감격해서 말했다.

"아, 어머니, 어머니! 저를 낳고 칠 일 만에 돌아가셔서 얼굴을 몰라보았어요. 불효를 용서해 주세요."

신선 taoist hermit | 영문 reason | 감격하다 to be deeply moved, to be touched

"그게 무슨 말이냐? 너를 두고 일찍 떠난 나를 용서해 주렴. 청아, 이렇게 보니 참으로 좋구나. 하루도 너를 보고 싶어 하지 않은 날이 없었다. 어디 보자. 이것은 내가 끼던 옥가락지가 아니냐. 말투며 생김새며 손가락에 낀 정표까지 내 딸 청이가 틀림없구나. 소중한 내 딸, 어미가 한번 안아 보자."

청이는 어머니의 품에 안겨 울며 말했다.

"어머니, 저도 어머니가 너무나 그리웠어요. 동네 아이들을 볼 때마다 저에게도 어머니가 있다면 얼마나 좋을까 생각했어요. 어머니 얼굴을 몰라 꿈에서도 그려 보지 못했는데 이렇게 뵙게 되니 꿈만 같아요."

"그랬구나. 그랬어. 우리 딸, 어미 없이 앞 못 보는 아비와 얼마나 고생을 많이 하였느냐."

"아니에요. 저는 이렇게 용궁에서 편히 지내며 돌아가신 어머니까지 만났는데 앞 못 보는 아버지는 어떻게 지내실지 걱정이네요."

그렇게 모녀는 오랜 시간 동안 못 다한 이야기를 나누었고 시간은 야속할 정도로 빠르게 흘러 곧 옥진 부인이 돌아갈 시간이 되었다.

"청아, 지금은 이 어미와 이별하지만 곧 네 아버지를 만나 웃는 날이 올 것이니 너무 슬퍼하지 말거라. 그리고 훗날 우리 세 식구가 모두 만날 날도 올 테니 그때 맘껏 정을 나누자꾸나."

그렇게 마지막 약속을 하고 옥진 부인은 하늘나라로 돌아갔다.

> V + -자꾸나: Expresses a suggestion, with a familiar manner, doing something together.

정표 keepsake, memento | 야속하다 to be cruel

7

심청, 연꽃 타고 황후가 되다

Track 07

호화로운 용궁 생활이었지만 홀로 계신 아버지와 헤어진 어머니 생각에 심청의 마음은 슬프기 그지없었다. 심청이 용궁에 온 지 삼 년이 되는 날, 옥황상제는 용왕에게 명을 내렸다.

> A + −기 그지없다: Written in the form −기(가) 그지없다, this expresses something that defies description.

"심청을 다시 인당수로 올려 보내 인간 세상에서 짝을 만나 부귀영화를 누리게 하라."

> 부귀영화(富貴榮華): Means to become esteemed by having a lot of wealth and high status, so as to enjoy all the glory in the whole world.

이에 용왕은 심청이 물 밖으로 안전하게 나갈 수 있도록 큰 연꽃 송이를 준비했다. 그리고 그 안에 온갖 패물을 실은 후 심청을 시녀 둘과 함께 태워 물 밖으로 올려 보냈다.

마침 심청을 제물로 바쳤던 뱃사람들도 남경에서 큰돈을 벌어 인당수를 지나가는 중이었다. 뱃사람 중 가장 나이 많은 이가 말했다.

"우리가 이렇게 억만금을 벌게 된 것은 다 심 낭자 덕분이네. 이제 인당수에 다다르니 고기와 술로 심 낭자의 넋을 달래 주세."

> V + −(으)세: Expresses a suggestion of doing something together. Often used colloquially.

호화롭다 to be luxurious, to be extravagant | **패물** jewels | **억만금** countless money | **다다르다** to reach, to arrive at | **넋** soul, spirit

그리하여 뱃사람들은 고기와 떡, 여러 가지 과일과 술을 한 상 가득 차려 놓고 심 낭자의 넋을 위로하기 위한 제사를 지냈다. 모두 심청을 희생시킨 것에 대해 미안한 마음이 컸다. 그렇게 제사를 지내던 그때 난데없이 커다란 분홍빛 연꽃 한 송이가 물 위로 둥실 떠올랐다. 엄청난 크기의 꽃이, 그것도 바다 한 가운데에서 갑자기 떠올랐으니 뱃사람들이 놀란 것은 당연했다.

"심 낭자의 넋이 꽃이 되어 나타난 것인가?"

"세상을 두루 다녔어도 이런 진귀한 꽃은 본 적이 없소."

"꽃에서 기이한 기운이 감도는 게 보통 꽃은 아닌 것 같소."

뱃사람들은 꽃을 조심스럽게 건져 올려 배에 실었다. 꽃을 싣고 보니 어찌 된 일인지 몇 달이 걸릴 길을 며칠 만에 도착할 수 있었다.

그때 이 나라 황제가 황후를 병으로 잃은 후 그 슬픔을 달래기 위해 매일 정원에서 황후가 좋아했던 꽃들을 바라본다는 소문이 전해졌다. 뱃사람들은 이 진귀한 꽃을 황제에게 바치기 위해 궁으로 가져갔다. 뱃사람들이 찬란하고 아름다운 연꽃을 황제에게 바치니 황제는 기뻐하며 이 꽃을 특별히 귀하게 여겼다.

난데없이 all of a sudden | **두루** throughout, widely | **진귀하다** to be rare and precious | **기이하다** to be strange, to be odd | **감돌다** to hang | **황후** empress | **찬란하다** to be radiant, to be brilliant

하루는 황제가 밤중에 산책하다가 연꽃 앞을 지나게 되었는데 연꽃에서 무슨 소리가 나는 것 같았다. 가까이 다가가 살펴보니 꽃잎 안쪽에 두 여인이 서 있는 것이 보였다. 두 사람은 바로 용왕이 심청과 함께 연꽃에 태웠던 시녀들이었다. 황제는 의아해하며 물었다.

"너희는 누구인데 그 안에 있느냐?"

시녀들은 그 자리에 선 채 황제의 물음에 답했다.

"저희는 옥황상제와 용왕의 명을 받아 심 낭자를 모시고 온 용궁의 시녀들입니다."

"대체 심 낭자가 누구냐?"

"하늘이 내린 효녀이신데 옥황상제께서 연분을 찾기 위해 이 세상에 보내셨습니다."

"옥황상제께서 내게 좋은 인연을 보내 주셨구나. 하늘이 내린 효녀라면 한번 만나 보고 싶다."

그러자 그때까지만 해도 살짝 오므라져 있던 연꽃 봉오리가 천천히 열리더니 아름다운 여인이 나왔다. 심청이었다. 그 모습이 어찌나 아름다운지 심청으로 인해 궁궐이 찬란한 빛에 휩싸였다.

의아하다 to be strange, to be odd | 연분 preordained bond/match | 오므라지다 to pucker |
봉오리 flower bud | 휩싸이다 to be filled, to be engulfed in

황제는 궁녀를 불러 심청을 극진히 모시도록 했다. 그리고 다음날 황제는 이 일을 신하들과 의논하였는데 모두가 심청을 옥황상제가 보내신 황후라고 생각하며 황제에게 국모로 맞이하기를 간청했다. 황제 역시 같은 생각이었기 때문에 길일에 혼례를 성대하게 치르기로 했다.

TIP! 길일: A day on which everything goes well. According to folk customs, days for moving house, weddings, etc., were decided based on auscipicous days.

혼례 준비는 빈틈없이 이루어졌고 어느덧 혼례 날이 되었다. 나라의 경사를 맞이하여 모든 신하와 백성들은 황제와 황후를 축하하며 기뻐 환호하였다.

심청이 황후가 되어 어진 성품으로 황제를 보필하고 궁의 일을 맡아 처리하니 해마다 풍년이고, 온 나라에 노랫소리가 끊이지 않는 태평성대가 이어졌다. 그러나 황후가 된 심청은 마음속으로 항상 아버지를 걱정하고 그리워하느라 하루도 마음 편히 지낼 수 없었다.

태평성대(太平聖代): Means a period of peace where there are no troubles in the land and the peasants live comfortably.

어느 날 심청이 혼자 흐느끼는 모습을 본 황제가 놀라 물었다.

"황후, 무슨 근심이라도 있으시오? 황후의 내조 덕분에 온 나라가 태평성대를 누리는데 황후는 무엇 때문에 그리 눈물을 흘리고 있소? 내게 말해 보시오."

궁녀 lady of the court | 국모 the mother of the state, empress, queen | 간청하다 to plead, to entreaty | 혼례 wedding | 성대하다 to be magnificent, to be grant | 빈틈없이 perfectly, missing nothing | 성품 one's nature/disposition | 보필하다 to assist, to help | 풍년 year of bountiful crops | 내조 support of a wife

그러자 심청은 그동안의 일들을 말하며 오랫동안 참아 온 눈물을 흘렸다.

"소첩은 원래 용궁 사람이 아니라, 황주 도화동에 사는 심학규의 딸 심청이라 합니다. | 소첩: A word used by a wife to lower herself before her husband. 아버지의 눈을 뜨게 하려고 인당수의 제물이 되었다가 옥황상제와 용왕님의 도움으로 여기까지 오게 되었습니다. 제가 비록 황후가 되어 남 부러울 것 없이 살고 있지만 고향에서 고생하실 아버지를 생각하면 마음 편한 날이 없기에 이렇게 남몰래 울었던 것입니다."

황제는 심청의 효심에 감동하여 심청을 따뜻하게 위로했다.

"그런 근심이 있었으면 진작 말해 주지 그랬소? 어렵지 않은 일이니 즉시 명을 내려 황후의 아버지를 찾도록 하겠소."

하지만 심학규는 일 년 전 고향 마을을 떠난 뒤 어디에 갔는지 모른다는 소식만이 전해졌다. 상심한 심청에게 황제가 말했다.

"황후, 너무 걱정하지 마시오. 살아 있기만 하다면 어떻게든 만날 수 있을 것이오."

그 말을 듣고 문득 떠오르는 생각이 있어 심청은 이렇게 말했다.

"저에게 좋은 방법이 하나 있습니다. 이 나라의 모든 맹인들을 불러 모아 잔치를 하면 어떻겠습니까? 그 속에 제 아버님이 있어 만날 수 있다면 제 소원을 풀 수 있을 것이고, 다른 맹인들도 맛난 음식을 먹으며 한을 풀 수 있으니 모두가 좋지 않겠습니까?"

남몰래 secretly | **상심하다** to grieve

심청의 말을 들은 황제는 크게 기뻐하며 칭찬하였다.

"그것 참 좋은 생각이오. 황후의 말처럼 전국의 맹인들을 모두 모아 잔치를 열도록 하라."

신하들은 전국 방방곡곡에 황제의 명을 전하며 한 사람도 빠짐없이 잔치에 참여할 것을 당부했다. 심청은 맹인 잔치가 열리는 날만을 손꼽아 기다렸다.

> 손꼽아 기다리다: To await with anticipation; this means that one counts down the days as one waits.

맹인 blind person | 방방곡곡 all throughout the land

<u>8</u>

심 봉사, 고난의 삶을 살다

Track 08

한편 심 봉사는 심청이 떠난 강가에 앉아 매일매일 통곡하며 지냈다. 심청의 목숨과 맞바꾼 공양미 삼백 석으로도 심 봉사는 아직 눈을 뜨지 못한 채였다.

"청아, 내 딸 청아! 내가 전생에 많은 죄를 지었나 보다. 금쪽같은 내 딸이 아비 눈 뜨게 하겠다고 스스로 저승길로 걸어갔는데, 그 아비는 눈도 못 뜨고 딸마저 잃었으니 내가 숨 쉬는 이곳이 지옥이다. 지옥이야."

> 금쪽같다: (lit. to be like gold) A figure of speech used to express that something is very precious and important.

혼자 밥을 차려 먹을 수도 없고, 빨래며 살림도 할 수 없으니 심 봉사의 몰골은 눈 뜨고 보기 힘들 정도가 되었다. 그때 아랫마을에 뺑덕 어미라는 여인이 심 봉사의 딱한 사정을 듣게 되었다. 뺑덕 어미는 심 봉사를 찾아가 따뜻한 밥도 지어 주고 집안일도 해 주며 가깝게 지냈다. 심 봉사는 뺑덕 어미에게 점차 의지하게 되었고 덕분에 심 봉사의 얼굴에 다시 살이 오르고 옷차림도 깔끔해졌다.

저승길 one's final journey (toward death) | **지옥** hell | **몰골** one's appearance | **살이 오르다** to put on weight

빵덕 어미가 싹싹하고 상냥하게 대해 주니 웃을 일 없을 것만 같던 그에게도 웃는 일이 생겼다.

'앞도 못 보고 아내와 자식까지 잃은 내게 이렇게 잘해 주니 고맙기 그지없다. 하늘이 내게 살길을 열어 주시려나 보다.'

결국 심 봉사는 빵덕 어미를 아내로 맞이했다. 하지만 그녀는 심 봉사의 생각처럼 좋은 사람이 아니었다. 사실 빵덕 어미는 장사꾼들이 심 봉사를 위해 공양미 삼백 석 외에도 돈과 곡식, 옷감을 부족함 없이 주고 갔다는 소문을 듣고 일부러 심 봉사를 찾아갔던 것이다. 심 봉사와 결혼한 빵덕 어미는 심 봉사의 재물을 물 쓰듯 했고 집안 살림을 돌보는 것도 뒷전이었다. 하루는 심 봉사가 빵덕 어미에게 물었다.

> 물 쓰듯 하다: (lit. to spend like water) A figure of speech indicating that money, objects, etc. are thoughtlessly being used very wastefully.

"빵덕 어미. 이웃 사람들 말이 우리 집 형편이 꽤 괜찮았었는데 지금은 쪽박 신세라 하오. 그게 정말인가?"

> 쪽박 신세: A figure of speech indicating a life of very difficult circumstances, to the degree that one must carry a bowl around to beg.

"대충 그러합니다."

"뭐? 그러하다고? 내 딸 청이가 팔려 갈 때 뱃사람들이 늙어서라도 편하게 지내라고 주고 간 것이 꽤 많았는데 그것들이 다 어디로 가고 없단 말이오?"

"어디로 가긴 어디로 가요. 다 써 버렸지."

싹싹하다 to be pleasant, to be affable | **상냥하다** to be kind, to be gentle | **뒷전** neglect

"뭐? 어디에?"

"쌀 팔아 떡 사 먹고, 의복 팔아 엿 사 먹고, 세간 팔아 술 사 먹었소. 이제 남아 있는 건 빚뿐이오."

뺑덕 어미가 뻔뻔스럽게 말했다. 심 봉사는 기가 막혔다.

"뭐? 그대는 양심도 없는가? 하긴 누굴 탓하겠는가. 딸이 아비 위해 남긴 재물도 간수 못한 내가 바보지. 다시 동냥해서 먹고 살려니 부끄러워 못 살겠네. 차라리 자네와 나, 함께 이 마을을 떠나세."

"그러고 싶으면 그렇게 합시다."

그리하여 남은 살림 다 팔아서 뺑덕 어미가 진 빚을 갚은 심 봉사는 빈 봇짐을 메고 뺑덕 어미와 함께 고향을 떠났다. 일 년이 지나고 새로 이사 간 마을의 사또가 심 봉사를 불렀다.

"궁에서 맹인 잔치를 연다고 하오. 여기 한양까지 갈 여비를 줄 테니 꼭 참석하도록 하시오."

심 봉사가 돈을 들고 좋아하며 집에 돌아와 뺑덕 어미를 불렀다.

"여보게, 뺑덕 어미. 황제께서 맹인들을 위해 잔치를 여신다고 하니 자네도 같이 가세. 이렇게 여비까지 받았으니 돈 걱정은 말게."

> V + -게: Expresses a command to a subordinate or someone familiar to make them do something or make a suggestion.

세간 furniture, household goods | 뻔뻔스럽다 to be shameless | 양심 conscience | 하긴 in truth, but then again | 간수하다 to store, to keep safe | 봇짐 bundle | 사또 magistrate | 여비 travel expenses

빼덕 어미는 심 봉사가 받아온 돈도 탐나고 한양 구경도 하고 싶어서 그러겠다고 대답했다. 그러나 빼덕 어미는 한양으로 가는 도중에 젊고 돈 많은 황 봉사를 만났다. 빼덕 어미는 곰곰이 생각했다.

'한양에 가 봐야 내가 잔치에 갈 수도 없고, 잔치가 끝나고 돌아와 봐야 형편도 예전만 못할 텐데……. 차라리 황 봉사를 따라가면 앞으로 더 편하게 살 수 있겠구나.'

빼덕 어미는 한양으로 가는 여비마저 훔쳐서는 황 봉사와 함께 사라져 버렸다.

탐(이) 나다 to covet | 곰곰이 thoughtfully, with care | 예전 the past, the old days

심 봉사는 신세 한탄을 했다.

"애고, 무정하고 고약한 사람. 해도 해도 너무하는구나.
도망치려면 날 궁에 데려다 놓고 도망칠 것이지. 낯선 곳에 와서
이게 웬일인가? 하긴 이 모두 내 팔자인 것을 누굴 탓해 무엇
하겠는가. 어진 곽 씨 보내고도 잘 살았고, 착한 딸 청이 보내고도
잘 살았는데 너 없다고 못 살겠느냐? 에잇! 잘 가거라."

혼자가 된 심 봉사는 터덜터덜 한양을 향해 걸었다. 넘어지고
떨어지고 부딪히기를 수십 번도 더 했다. 그래도 하늘의 도움이
있었는지 죽지 않고 살아 심 봉사는 한양에 도착할 수 있었다.
심 봉사는 맹인 잔치가 끝나는 마지막 날에 이름과 고향을 적어
낸 후 간신히 잔치에 참석했다.

신세 한탄 lamentation over one's misfortune | 무정하다 to be cold, to be cruel | 고약하다 to be foul,
to be nasty | 팔자 destiny, fate | 터덜터덜 trudging

9
심 봉사, 눈을 뜨다

Track 09

한편 심청은 잔치의 마지막 날이 되자 안절부절못했다.

'오늘이 마지막 잔칫날인데 아버지는 보이지 않는구나. 혹시 부처님의 은혜로 눈을 뜨신 것일까? 늙고 병들어 한양까지 못 오시는 것일까? 아니면 불효자식 보내고 속 끓이다 세상을 떠나신 것일까? 불쌍한 우리 아버지, 알 길이 없으니 답답하구나.'

심청은 조급한 마음에 직접 맹인 잔치에 나가 살펴봐야겠다고 생각했다. 그때 내관이 급히 달려와 말하였다.

"심학규라는 맹인이 방금 장부에 이름을 적었나이다."

> 내관(內官): A government official who escorts the ruler and protects the crown during a night shift.

황제는 바로 그 맹인을 모셔오도록 했다. 심청은 두근거리는 가슴을 진정시키며 기다렸다. 잠시 후 맹인 한 사람이 황제와 황후 앞에 섰다. 내관이 황제와 황후가 앞에 계신다고 알려 주니 맹인은 엎드려 절하며 황송해했다. 황제가 물었다.

"어디에서 온 맹인인가?"

안절부절못하다 to feel restless and uneasy, to be in a state of being at a loss at what to do | **불효자식** undutiful child | **속 끓이다** to be anxious, to worry | **조급하다** to be impatient | **황송하다** to be grateful

맹인이 황제의 물음에 답했다.

"저는 처자식도 없고 거처하는 곳도 없는 불쌍한 맹인이옵니다."

심청은 심 봉사의 초라한 모습에서 옛 모습을 찾아보기 힘들어 물었다.

> N + (이)옵니다: An old form of speech used to very politely describe a fact to another person.

"맹인은 다시 성명과 거주지 그리고 처자식에 대해 자세히 밝히시오."

심 봉사는 처자식이라는 말이 나오자 슬픔을 감당할 수 없어 눈물을 흘리며 말했다.

"소인의 고향은 황주 도화동이고 성은 심, 이름은 학규라 하옵니다. 곽 씨 집안의 여인을 아내로

> 소인: A first-person pronoun used by someone of low social standing to speak to someone of a higher social standing, lowering oneself.

맞았는데 스물이 되어 눈이 멀었습니다. 눈 먼 남편 보살피느라 고생만 한 아내는 마흔에 세상을 떠났고 아내가 남기고 간 딸 아이 하나를 젖동냥으로 근근이 길렀습니다. 그런데 그만 그 딸이 제 눈을 뜨게 하려고 공양미 삼백 석에 몸을 팔아 인당수에서 죽었나이다. 그런데도 눈도 뜨지 못하고 자식만 죽였으니 이렇게 사는 것이 죽는 것보다 못합니다. 딸을 죽인 죄인을 죽여 주시옵소서."

처자식 one's wife and children | **거처하다** to reside | **초라하다** to be poor, to be shabby | **근근이** barely

이 말을 들은 심 황후는 버선발로 달려가 아버지의 목을 잡고
통곡했다.

"아이고, 아버지! 어찌 여태 눈을 뜨지 못하셨어요. 뱃사람들이
재물을 남겼건만 무슨 고생을 하셨기에 이리 늙으셨어요. 인당수에
빠져 죽었던 심청이가 이렇게
살아왔으니 어서 눈을 떠서
청이를 좀 보세요, 아버지."

> V + –건만: A shortened form of –건마는 used when the clause that follows is the opposite of the anticipated result or situation of the preceding clause.

"뭐? 청이? 우리 청이? 아니, 죽었던 우리 청이가 살아왔단
말이냐? 이게 꿈이냐 생시냐?"

> 꿈이냐 생시냐: (lit. is this a dream or is this reality?) Used when something one wished for ardently suddenly comes true to express that it feels like a dream.

"네, 아버지. 청이에요.
아버지의 하나뿐인 딸 청이에요."

심 봉사는 더듬더듬 심 황후의 얼굴을 만져보고, 목소리를
들어봐도 알 수 없으니 답답해 미칠 것만 같았다.

"아이고, 청아! 답답해 못 견디겠다! 어디 한번 보자꾸나! 내 딸
얼굴 좀 보고 싶다!"

심 봉사가 눈을 있는 힘껏 뜨려 애쓰며 가슴의 한을 담아 고래고래
소리 질렀다. 그런데 이게 무슨 일인지, 갑자기 심 봉사의 두 눈이
번쩍 뜨이며 앞이 밝아졌다. 그리고 곧 심 봉사의 눈에 심청의
얼굴이 비쳤다.

고래고래 loudly | 번쩍 easily and widely | 뜨이다 to be opened

"청아, 청아! 보인다. 네가 보인다! 선녀처럼 고운 네가 보인다! 네가 정말 내 딸 청이란 말이냐?"

"네? 아버지, 정말 제가 보이세요? 아아, 아버지! 저는 인당수에서 꼼짝없이 죽는 줄로만 알았어요. 그런데 이렇게 살아 아버지를 뵙고, 아버지가 눈도 뜨셨으니 저는 이제 죽어도 여한이 없어요."

"내 사랑하는 딸아, 죽는다는 말은 다시는 하지 말거라. 그런데 이 옷은 다 무엇이며, 네가 왜 궁에 있느냐?"

심 봉사가 뒤늦게 정신을 차리고 물었다.

"아버지, 저는 옥황상제님의 은혜로 이렇게 황후가 되었어요."

"뭐? 내 딸이 황후가 되다니! 네 효심에 하늘이 감동하여 복을 주셨구나!"

> V + -다니: Expresses feelings such as surprises, admiration, indignation, regret, etc. as realizing a fact. Often used colloquially.

심 봉사가 심청을 부여잡고 덩실덩실 춤을 추니 모여 있던 사람들이 이 광경을 보고 자기의 일처럼 기뻐했다. 심 봉사가 눈을 떠서 춤추고 노래하는 소리가 천하에 쩌렁쩌렁 울려 퍼져 온 나라의 맹인들도 그 소리를 듣고 일시에 눈을 떴다. 맹인 잔치 동안 먼저 왔다가 돌아간 맹인들도 집에서 눈을 뜨고, 길 위에서도 눈을 뜬다. 온 나라의 맹인들이 제각기 눈을 뜨니 온 나라에 놀라는 소리가 또 한 번 떠들썩하였다. 심 황후의 어진 덕으로 온 세상에 눈먼 사람들이 모두 세상의 빛을 보았다고 백성들이 입을 모아 칭찬하였다.

꼼짝없이 helplessly | **여한** regret | **부여잡다** to grab, to clutch at | **덩실덩실** joyfully (a mimetic word describing in the manner of dancing with joy) | **쩌렁쩌렁** resonantly (an onomatopeic word of the loud and resonant sound) | **일시에** all at once | **제각기** each

심 황후는 아버지를 예복으로 갈아입게 하고 예를 다해 내전으로 모셨다. 그런 후에 심 봉사와 마주 앉아 여러 해 동안 쌓인 이야기를 몇 날 며칠 하는데, 한 번 웃으면 한 번 울고 하며 그리던 정을 나누었다. 심 황후의 지극한 효심을 온 백성이 두고두고 칭송하며 본받으니 태평성대가 끝이 없었다.

예복 formal clothing | **내전** queen's residence in a palace | **그리다** to miss | **지극하다** to be extreme, to be utmost | **칭송하다** to praise | **본받다** to emulate, to model oneself after

부록
Appendix

1

1 빈칸에 알맞은 단어를 넣어 대화를 완성하세요.

Put the correct word in each blank to complete the dialogues.

기울다	후손	남녀노소	부양하다

(1) 가 우리 (   )에게 깨끗하고 아름다운 자연환경을 물려주어야 할 의무가
있다고 생각합니다.

　　나 네, 말씀 감사합니다.

(2) 가 주인공으로 출연하신 영화가 이번 크리스마스에 개봉한다면서요?
영화 소개 간단히 부탁드릴게요.

　　나 네, 이 영화는 (   ) 누구나 좋아할 만한 감동적인 내용입니다.
오셔서 가족들과 즐겁게 관람하세요.

(3) 가 김 교수님을 가장 존경한다고 하셨다면서요?

　　나 네, 어릴 때 저희 집 형편이 갑자기 (   ) 많이 힘들었는데 교수님
덕분에 이겨낼 수 있었거든요.

(4) 가 어린 나이에 부모님 없이 동생들을 (   ) 것이 참 어려웠을 텐데요.

　　나 네, 당시 제가 고등학생이었는데, 학업을 중단하고 일을 하기 시작했습니다.

2 다음 중 알맞지 않은 부분을 찾아 바르게 고치세요.

Find the incorrect sections and correct them.

(1) 곽 씨는 입이 닳도록 삯바느질을 했다.

➡ _____

(2) 부부는 아이가 없어 대가 이어지게 생겼다.

➡ _____

(3) 부부는 아이 생각만 하면 좋아서 입이 짧아졌다.

➡ _____

(4) 심 봉사는 갑자기 좋은 생각이 떠올라 무릎을 탁 꿇으며 말했다.

➡ _____

3 이야기의 내용과 맞으면 ○, 틀리면 ✕ 표시하세요.

Mark ○ if the statement is true, and mark ✕ if it is false.

(1) 심 봉사와 곽 씨는 같은 꿈을 꾸었다.　　　　　　　　(　)

(2) 부부는 자식을 갖게 해 달라고 빌었다.　　　　　　　(　)

(3) 심 봉사는 아이가 아들이 아니라서 실망했다.　　　　(　)

(4) 부부는 아이가 태어나기 전부터 이름을 정해 두었다.　(　)

4 태몽의 내용이 <u>아닌</u> 것은 무엇입니까?

Which of the following is not a part of the conception dream?

① 선녀가 학을 타고 내려왔다.　　　② 하늘에 오색구름이 펼쳐졌다.

③ 집안에 향기로운 냄새가 가득했다.　④ 선녀가 옥으로 만든 노리개를 주고 떠났다.

5 다음 질문에 알맞은 답을 쓰세요.

Write the correct answer for each of the following questions.

(1) 글에서 나타난 심 봉사와 곽 씨의 성격을 나타내는 말을 찾아 쓰세요.

어질다	현명하다	군자와 같다	마음이 곧다
기품이 있다	행동이 바르다	마음씨가 곱다	

①

심 봉사

곽 씨

②

(2) 곽 씨가 죽기 전 남긴 유언 두 가지는 무엇인가요?

① _____

② _____

2

1 [보기]와 같이 다음 글의 밑줄 친 단어를 의미가 비슷한 다른 단어로 바꾸어 보세요.
As in the example, change the underlined word to a different word with the same meaning.

> 보기　"옆집 부인이 <u>해산한 지</u> 며칠 되지 않았으니 내가 부탁하여 보겠소."
> → 아이를 낳은 지

(1) 동네 아낙네들은 심 봉사와 심청 부녀를 <u>딱하게</u> <u>여겼다</u>.
　　　　　　　　　　　　　　　　　　　　　　　　①　　　②

① _____　　② _____

(2) "<u>혹여</u> 남는 밥을 나눠 주신다면 추운 날 찬 방에서 기다리시는 <u>부친</u>께서
　　①　　　　　　　　　　　　　　　　　　　　　　　　　　　　　　　　②

<u>허기</u>를 <u>면할</u> 수 있겠나이다."
　③　　　④

① _____　　② _____

③ _____　　④ _____

2 **빈칸에 알맞은 단어를 넣어 문장을 완성하세요.**

Put the correct word in each blank to complete the sentences.

구걸하다	어르다	알뜰하다	끼니

(1) 우는 청이를 밤새 (　　　　　) 심 봉사는 아침이 되자 젖동냥을 하러 갔다.

(2) 심 봉사는 이 집 저 집으로 쌀을 (　　　　　) 다녔다.

(3) 심청은 삯바느질을 하여 (　　　　　) 돈을 모았다.

(4) 심청의 노력 덕분에 부녀가 충분히 (　　　　　)를 해결할 수 있었다.

3 **어울리는 것끼리 연결하여 문장을 만드세요.**

Connect the phrases that go together to create complete sentences.

(1) 부인을 잃은 심봉사는　·　　　　　　·　① 도가 텄다.

(2) 동네 아낙들도 청이에게　·　　　　　　·　② 궁리해 주었다.
　　젖 먹일 방도를

(3) 처음이 어렵지 심 봉사는　·　　　　　　·　③ 하늘이 무너지는 것 같았다.
　　점점 젖동냥에

4 **다음 중 이야기의 내용과 같은 것은 무엇입니까?**

Which of the following matches the context of the story?

① 심청은 가난한 아버지를 원망했다.

② 심청은 어머니를 닮아 바느질을 잘했다.

③ 심청은 밥을 얻으러 나갔다가 넘어져 다쳤다.

④ 심청은 심 봉사의 반대로 밥을 얻으러 다닐 수 없었다.

5   **다음 질문에 알맞은 답을 쓰세요.**

Write the correct answer for each of the following questions.

(1) 심청이 심 봉사 대신 밥을 얻으러 가겠다고 부탁할 때 예를 들어 한 이야기는 무엇입니까?

_____

_____

_____

_____

(2) 다음은 심청이 겨울에 먹을 것을 얻으러 나선 모습입니다. 심청의 모습을 묘사해 보세요.

_____

_____

_____

_____

<u>3</u>

1 **다음 빈칸에 알맞은 단어를 넣으세요.**

Put the correct word in the crossword puzzle.

(1)	(2)					
				(4)		
			(3)			
(5)	(6)	(8)				
		(7)				
					(10)	
				(9)		

가로

(1) 승상 부인은 심청이 마음에 들어 ○○○로 삼고 싶어 했다.

(3) 심 봉사는 심청에게 ○○○○에 어긋나지 않게 행동하라고 말했다.

(5) 승상 부인은 심청이 듣던 대로 ○○○○고 생각했다.

(7) 승상 부인은 심청에게 자신이 ○○ 부탁을 했으니 섭섭하게 생각하지 말아 달라고 했다.

(9) "어서 '심학규 쌀 삼백 석'이라고 시주 ○○에 적어 내 눈을 뜨게 해 주십시오."

세로

(2) 승상 부인은 심청에게 옷감과 ○○을 싸 주었다.

(4) 승상 부인은 일찍이 남편을 ○○○ 혼자 살고 있었다.

(6) "사람 살려! 거기 아무도 없소? ○○○○, 이게 웬 날벼락이냐!"

(8) 심청은 승상 부인과 수도 놓고 ○○도 먹으며 이야기를 나누었다.

(10) 심 봉사는 심청에게 조심히 잘 다녀오라고 ○○했다.

2 다음 문장의 의미로 알맞은 것을 고르세요.
Choose the correct meaning of the following sentence.

집의 규모와 화려함이 비길 데가 없었다.

① 집이 규모에 비해 화려하지 않다.

② 집은 화려하지만 규모는 크지 않다.

③ 다른 집과 비교했을 때 집이 작고 평범하다.

④ 비교 대상을 찾을 수 없을 정도로 집이 크고 화려하다.

3 빈칸에 알맞은 말을 넣어 문장을 완성하세요.
Put the correct expression in each blank to complete the sentences.

마음에 걸리다   눈이 휘둥그레지다
입이 닳다   버선발로 뛰어나오다

(1) 효성스러운 심청을 보고 마을 사람들은 (　　　　　　　　) 칭찬했다.

(2) 심청은 아버지를 혼자 두고 승상 댁에 가는 것이 (　　　　　　).

(3) 심청은 대궐 같은 집을 보고 (　　　　　　).

(4) 기다리던 심청이 도착했다는 말을 듣고 승상 부인은 반가워서 (　　　　　　).

4 장 승상 부인에 대한 설명으로 알맞지 않은 것을 고르세요.
Choose the in correct description of Prime Minister Jang's wife.

① 화려하고 큰 집에서 혼자 살았다.

② 심청을 딸로 맞아 함께 지내고 싶어 했다.

③ 심청의 예의 바른 행동과 말씨를 마음에 들어 했다.

④ 남편과 아들들이 모두 한양에서 벼슬살이를 하고 있었다.

5 다음 질문에 알맞은 답을 쓰세요.

Write the correct answer for each of the following questions.

(1) 심 봉사가 물에 빠진 이유는 무엇입니까?

_____

_____

_____

(2) 승려는 심 봉사가 눈을 뜰 수 있는 방법을 무엇이라 말했습니까?

_____

_____

_____

4

1 다음 문장에 어울리는 단어를 찾아 ○ 표시하세요.

Circle the word that best suits each of the following sentences.

(1) 심 봉사는 (내막 / 대책) 없이 공양미 삼백 석을 약속한 자신의 행동을 후회했다.

(2) 아버지, 왜 진지를 안 드세요? 무슨 (이익 / 근심)이라도 있으세요?

(3) 부처님 앞에 약속하고 후회하면 (효험 / 효심)이 없어요.

(4) 심청이 몸을 팔기로 (언약하자 / 털어놓자) 뱃사람들은 공양미 삼백 석을 몽은사에 보냈다.

2 **다음 표현의 의미를 바르게 연결하세요.**
Connect each expression with the correct meaning.

(1) 경거망동하다   •

(2) 귀가 번쩍 뜨이다   •

(3) 지성이면 감천이다   •

(4) 냄새가 코를 찌르다   •

(5) 가슴이 찢어질 듯하다   •

• ① 경솔하여 조심성 없이 행동하다

• ② 냄새가 후각을 세게 자극하다

• ③ 가슴에 고통이 느껴질 정도로 슬픔이 크다

• ④ 무슨 일이든지 정성을 다하면 어려운 일도 이룰 수 있다

• ⑤ 어떤 말이나 이야기가 무척 그럴듯해 선뜻 마음이 끌리다

3 **다음에 알맞은 단어를 넣어 문장을 완성하세요.**
Put the correct word in each blank to complete the sentences.

짓다	바치다	치르다	장만하다

(1) 심청은 서둘러 부엌으로 가서 저녁을 (　　　　　　　).

(2) 심청은 몸을 (　　　　　　　) 아버지의 눈을 뜨게 하고 싶었다.

(3) 집안이 가난하여 공양미 삼백 석을 (　　　　　　　) 방법이 없었다.

(4) 뱃사람은 심청과 약속을 하고 즉시 원하는 값을 (　　　　　　　).

4 **다음 중 이야기의 내용과 같은 것은 무엇입니까?**
Which of the following matches the content of the story?

① 장사꾼들의 배는 다음 달 5일에 떠난다.

② 심 봉사는 맛있는 반찬 냄새에 기분이 다시 좋아졌다.

③ 심청은 시주 장부에서 아버지의 이름을 지워 달라고 빌었다.

④ 심 봉사는 자신의 성급한 행동을 후회했고 심청은 아버지를 위로했다.

5 **다음 질문에 알맞은 답을 쓰세요.**
Write the correct answer for each of the following questions.

(1) 뱃사람들은 어떤 사람을 찾고 있습니까?

_____

_____

(2) 뱃사람들이 사람을 사려는 이유는 무엇입니까?

_____

_____

<u>**5**</u>

1 **빈칸에 알맞은 단어를 넣어 대화를 완성하세요.**
Put the correct word in each blank to complete the dialogues.

광풍	선뜻	철따라	출항하다

(1) 가 배가 언제쯤 도착할까?

나 2시간 전에 부산에서 (　　　　　　　) 곧 도착할 거야.

(2) 가 이번 모금 운동에 이렇게 (　　　　　　　) 나서 주셔서 감사합니다.

나 아닙니다. 좋은 일에 참여하게 되어 기쁩니다.

(3) 가 전원생활이 어때요?

나 좋아요. 도시에서 살 때는 몰랐는데 (　　　　　　　) 바뀌는 산과 들의 모습이
참 아름답더라고요.

(4) 가 오늘 뉴스에서 봤는데 (　　　　　　　) 때문에 가로수가 넘어져 도로를 덮쳤대.

나 그래? 인명 피해가 없어야 할 텐데 걱정이다.

2 빈칸에 알맞은 단어를 넣어 문장을 완성하세요.

Put the correct word in each blank to complete the sentences.

일다	이루다	마주하다	인자하다

(1) 심 봉사는 심청이 (   ) 장승 부인을 어머니로 모실 수 있어 잘되었다고
생각했다.

(2) 심청은 약속한 날이 다가오자 잠을 (   ) 수가 없었다.

(3) 아버지와 밥상을 (   ) 심청은 눈물이 났다.

(4) 인당수에 도착하자 파도가 세게 (   ).

3 다음은 심청이 누구에게 한 말입니까? 알맞게 연결하세요.

To whom does Sim Cheong say the following? Connect the correct answers.

(1) 장사꾼에게 ·　　　　　　　　· ① "부디 빨리 눈을 뜨시고
　　　　　　　　　　　　　　　　평안히 사세요."

(2) 심 봉사에게 ·　　　　　　　　· ② "아버님께 마지막 진지를 지어
　　　　　　　　　　　　　　　　올릴 시간을 주세요."

(3) 동네 사람들에게 ·　　　　　　· ③ "그동안 도와주신 은혜를 다 갚지
　　　　　　　　　　　　　　　　못하고 떠나 죄송합니다."

4 이야기의 내용과 맞으면 ○, 틀리면 × 표시하세요.

Mark ○ if the statement is true, and mark × if it is false.

(1) 승상 부인이 심청에게 공양미 삼백 석을 주었다. (　　)

(2) 심청이 인당수에 몸을 던지자 물결이 잠잠해졌다. (　　)

(3) 배는 출발한 지 5일째 되는 날 인당수에 도착했다. (　　)

(4) 심 봉사는 꿈을 통해 심청이 죽을 것임을 짐작했다. (　　)

5   다음 중 그림에 대한 묘사로 맞지 <u>않는</u> 것을 고르세요.

Choose the answer that does not describe the following picture.

① 하늘에서 굵은 빗줄기가 쏟아진다.

② 파도가 잠잠하고 바다는 고요하다.

③ 뱃사람들이 고사를 지내고 있다.

④ 심청이 뱃머리에 올라서서 두 손을 모은 채 빌고 있다.

6   다음 질문에 알맞은 답을 쓰세요.

Write the correct answer for each of the following questions.

(1) 심청은 혼자 남을 아버지를 위해 어떤 일을 해 두었습니까?

① _____

② _____

③ _____

(2) 심청은 인당수에 빠지기 전 뱃머리에 올라 무엇을 빌었습니까?

① 하느님께: _____

② 아버지를 위해: _____

<u>6</u>

1 다음 문장에 들어갈 단어를 찾아 ○ 표시하세요.

Circle the word that best suits each of the following sentences.

(1) 옥황상제는 용왕에게 심청을 궁에 모시라는 (명 / 죄)을/를 내렸다.

(2) 심청은 자신이 멀쩡히 살아서 아름다운 바닷속 궁궐에 있다는 것이

(당황했다 / 황당했다).

(3) 심청은 자신의 손을 잡는 옥진 부인을 보고 (시중 / 영문)을 몰라 어리둥절했다.

(4) 옥진 부인은 참았던 눈물을 (빠뜨리며 / 터트리며) 심청의 이름을 불렀다.

2 다음은 심청과 헤어지기 전 옥진 부인이 한 말입니다. 빈칸에 알맞은 단어를 넣어 글을 완성하세요.

The following is what Lady Okjin says before parting with Sim Cheong. Put the correct word in each blank to complete the passage.

| 맘껏 | 훗날 | 나누다 | 이별하다 |

"청아, 지금은 이 어미와 (1) (   )지만

곧 네 아버지를 만나 웃는 날이 올 것이니

너무 슬퍼하지 말거라. 그리고 (2) (   )

우리 세 식구가 모두 만날 날도 올 테니 그때

(3) (   ) 정을 (4) (   )자꾸나."

3 다음 중 '호의호식'을 바르게 설명한 것을 고르세요.

Choose which of the following correctly describes "호의호식."

① 온전하고 정상적인 상태

② 부족함 없이 풍요롭게 살아가는 모습

③ 매우 좋아서 현실이 아닌 것 같은 상태

④ 어떤 대상에 대하여 정성을 다하는 모습

4 글의 내용과 <u>다른</u> 것은 무엇입니까?

Choose the answer that does not match the content of the story.

① 심청은 용궁에서 극진한 대접을 받았다.

② 심청은 아버지에 대한 걱정으로 편히 지낼 수 없었다.

③ 심청은 용왕에게 어머니를 만나게 해 달라고 부탁했다.

④ 옥황상제는 3년 후 심청을 인간 세상으로 돌려보내라고 했다.

5 다음 질문에 알맞은 답을 쓰세요.

Write the correct answer for each of the following questions.

(1) 옥진 부인은 무엇을 보고 심청이 자신의 딸이 틀림없다고 했습니까? (3가지)

① _____

② _____

③ _____

(2) 심청은 언제 어머니가 그리웠다고 했습니까?

_____

_____

7

1 빈칸에 알맞은 단어를 넣어 대화를 완성하세요.

Put the correct word in each blank to complete the dialogues.

두루	풍년	억만금	성대하다

(1) 가 이 집은 무슨 일이 있어도 팔지 않을 거야. 내가 태어나 자란 곳이어서 추억이 많거든.

　　 나 그래. 그 추억은 (　　　　　　)을/를 준다고 해도 바꿀 수 없는 것이지.

(2) 가 이번 방학 때는 뭘 할 거야?

　　 나 국내 여러 곳을 (　　　　　　) 여행하며 많은 경험을 쌓고 싶어.

(3) 가 어제 부산국제영화제 개막식 봤어요?

　　 나 정말 (　　　　　　) 개막식이었어요. 현장에 없었던 게 아쉬워요.

(4) 가 작년엔 많이 가물었었는데 올해는 비가 넉넉하게 오네요.

　　 나 네, 올해는 농사가 잘 되어 (　　　　　　)이/가 들 것 같아요.

2 빈칸에 알맞은 단어를 넣어 문장을 완성하세요.

Put the correct word in each blank to complete the sentences.

넋	마르다	난데없이	오므라지다

(1) 심청은 아버지와 어머니 생각에 눈물이 (　　　　　　) 날이 없었다.

(2) 뱃사람들은 심청의 (　　　　　　)을/를 위로하기 위한 제사를 지냈다.

(3) 뱃사람들이 제사를 지내고 있을 때 (　　　　　　) 큰 연꽃 한 송이가 수면 위로 떠올랐다.

(4) (　　　　　　) 있던 연꽃 봉오리가 열리더니 아름다운 여인이 걸어 나왔다.

3 다음 말이 의미하는 것을 바르게 연결하세요.

Connect each of the following words to the correct meaning.

(1) 방방곡곡 ・   ・ ① 한 군데도 빠짐이 없는 모든 곳

(2) 부귀영화 ・   ・ ② 나라에 혼란이 없어 백성들이
                                  편안히 지내는 시대

(3) 태평성대 ・   ・ ③ 재산이 많고 지위가 높으며 귀하게 되어
                                  세상의 온갖 영광을 누리는 것

4 이야기의 내용과 맞으면 ○, 틀리면 × 표시하세요.

Mark ○ if the statement is true, and mark × if it is false.

(1) 심청은 수궁에서 3년 동안 있었다.   (   )

(2) 심청을 태운 연꽃을 뱃사람들이 발견했다.   (   )

(3) 신하들은 심청을 국모로 맞는 것에 반대했다.   (   )

(4) 황제는 심청이 심 봉사의 딸이라는 것을 알고 있었다.   (   )

5 글에 나타난 황제에게 바친 연꽃의 특징으로 맞는 것을 모두 골라 ○ 하세요.

Circle all of the following that appeared in the text as characteristics of the lotus blossom presented to the emperor.

커다랗다   흰색이다   진귀하다

아름답다   찬란하다   향기롭다

활짝 피었다   기이한 기운이 감돈다

6 다음 질문에 알맞은 답을 쓰세요.

Write the correct answer for each of the following questions.

(1) 용왕이 연꽃 안에 실은 세 가지는 무엇입니까?

① _____

② _____

③ _____

(2) 심 봉사를 찾기 위해서 심청은 어떤 방법을 제안했습니까?

_____

_____

8

1 다음 문장에 어울리는 단어를 찾아 ○ 표시하세요.

Circle the word that best suits each of the following sentences.

(1) 심 봉사는 심청이 떠난 강가에 앉아 (감격하며 / 통곡하며) 지냈다.

(2) 혼자 지내는 심 봉사의 (몰골 / 양심)은 눈 뜨고 보기 힘들 정도가 되었다.

(3) 뺑덕 어미 덕에 심 봉사의 얼굴에 다시 살이 (막혔다 / 올랐다).

(4) 심 봉사는 심청이 남긴 재물을 (간수하지/ 건사하지) 못한 자신이 바보 같았다.

2 다음은 심청을 떠나보낸 심 봉사의 한탄입니다. 빈칸에 알맞은 단어를 넣어 글을 완성하세요.

The following is the lament of Blind Man Sim after losing Sim Cheong. Put the correct word in each blank to complete the passage.

죄	전생	저승길	금쪽같다

"청아! 내가 (1) (   )에 많은 (2) (   )
을/를 지었었나 보다. (3) (   ) 내 딸이 아비 눈
뜨게 하겠다고 스스로 (4) (   )(으)로 걸어갔는데,
그 아비는 눈도 못 뜨고 딸마저 잃었으니 내가 숨 쉬는 이곳이
지옥이다. 지옥이야."

3 다음 중 뺑덕 어미에 대한 설명으로 알맞지 <u>않은</u> 것을 고르세요.

Choose the incorrect description of Bbaengdeok's mother.

① 살림을 팔아 빚을 갚았다.

② 한양으로 가는 여비를 훔쳤다.

③ 심 봉사의 재물을 물 쓰듯 했다.

④ 집안 살림을 돌보는 일은 뒷전이었다.

4 다음 중 이야기의 내용과 같은 것은 무엇입니까?

Which of the following matches the content of the story?

① 심 봉사는 결국 맹인 잔치에 참석하지 못했다.

② 사또는 심 봉사에게 맹인 잔치에 갈 여비를 주었다.

③ 동네 사람들이 혼자 된 심 봉사에게 돈과 곡식을 주었다.

④ 쪽박 신세가 된 심 봉사는 부끄러웠지만 고향을 떠나지 못했다.

5 결혼 전과 후, 뺑덕 어미의 심 봉사를 대하는 태도와 성격은 어떻게 달라졌는지 쓰세요.

Write how Bbaengdeok's mother's personality and the way she treats Blind Man Sim change before and after their marriage.

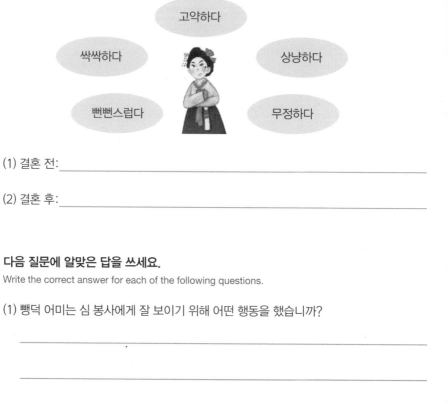

(1) 결혼 전: _____

(2) 결혼 후: _____

6 다음 질문에 알맞은 답을 쓰세요.

Write the correct answer for each of the following questions.

(1) 뺑덕 어미는 심 봉사에게 잘 보이기 위해 어떤 행동을 했습니까?

_____

_____

_____

(2) 뺑덕 어미가 심 봉사와 맹인 잔치에 함께 간 이유는 무엇입니까?

_____

_____

_____

<u>9</u>

1 다음 제시된 단어의 의미를 잘못 설명한 것을 고르세요.

Choose which of the following incorrectly describes the meaning of the word or phrase.

① 속 끓이다: 무엇에 크게 감동을 받은 모습

② 내관: 숙직을 하면서 임금을 모시며 관을 지키던 관원

③ 고래고래: 목소리를 높여 시끄럽게 외치거나 지르는 모양

④ 안절부절못하다: 마음이 초조하고 불안하여 어찌할 바를 모르는 상태

2 빈칸에 알맞은 단어를 넣어 문장을 완성하세요.

Put the correct word in each blank to complete the sentences.

번쩍	본받다	두고두고	조급하다

(1) 심 황후는 (　　　　　　) 마음에 직접 맹인 잔치에 나가 보았다.

(2) 심 봉사의 두 눈이 (　　　　　　) 뜨이며 앞이 밝아졌다.

(3) 심 황후의 효심을 온 백성이 (　　　　　　).

(4) 백성들은 심 황후를 (　　　　　　) 칭송했다.

3 사건이 일어난 순서에 맞게 문장을 나열하세요.

Arrange the sentences in the correct order in which they occurred.

> ㉠ 죽었던 청이가 살아왔다는 말에 심 봉사는 눈을 뜨려 애썼다.
> ㉡ 갑자기 심 봉사의 두 눈이 번쩍 뜨이며 앞을 볼 수 있게 되었다.
> ㉢ 심 황후는 심 봉사에게 이름과 사는 곳, 아내와 자식에 대해 물었다.
> ㉣ 심 봉사의 말을 들은 심 황후가 울며 아버지에게 자신이 심청임을 밝혔다.
> ㉤ 내관이 심학규라는 맹인이 장부에 이름을 적었음을 황제와 황후에게 알렸다.

_____ → _____ → _____ → _____ → _____

4 다음 질문에 알맞은 답을 쓰세요.

Write the correct answer for each of the following questions.

(1) 심청이 죽어도 여한이 없다고 말한 이유는 무엇입니까?

_____

_____

(2) 심청이 황후가 되었다는 말을 듣고 심 봉사가 한 행동은 무엇입니까?

_____

_____

1 ~ 9

1 다음은 '심청전'의 줄거리입니다. 빈칸에 알맞은 단어를 골라 쓰세요.

The following is a summary of "The Story of Sim Cheong." Put correct word in each blank.

연꽃	제물	효심	뜨다
벗어나다	바치다	여의다	칭송하다

심청은 어려서 어머니를 (1) (   ), 눈먼 아버지 밑에서 자랐다.
심청의 아버지 심 봉사는 공양미 삼백 석을 부처님께 (2) (   )
눈을 뜰 수 있다는 말에 시주를 약속했다. (3) (   )이/가 지극한
심청은 집안이 가난하여 공양미 삼백 석을 마련할 길이 없자, 남경 상인들에게
자신의 몸을 팔아 인당수의 (4) (   )이/가 되기로 했다. 인당수에
빠진 심청은 옥황상제와 용왕의 도움으로 죽을 위기에서 (5) (   ).
수궁에서 지냈는데 이곳에서 돌아가신 어머니를 만나게 되었다. 3년 뒤 용왕은

(6) (   )에 심청을 태워 바다 위로 올려 보냈고 이를 남경 상인들이
발견하여 황제에게 바쳤다. 황제는 연꽃에서 나온 심청을 황후로 맞이했고,
아버지를 그리워하는 심청을 위해 맹인 잔치를 열어 전국의 맹인들이 궁으로
모이게 하였다. 심청이 인당수로 떠난 후 온갖 고생을 한 심 봉사는 맹인
잔치에서 심청을 다시 만난 기쁨에 두 눈을 번쩍 (7) (   ). 이후 온
백성이 심청의 효심을 (8) (   ) 본받았다.

2   심청은 아버지의 눈을 뜨게 하려고 죽음을 선택했습니다. 심청의 이러한 행동을 '효'라고
할 수 있을까요? 여러분이 심청이라면 어떻게 행동했을까요?
Sim Cheong chose death in order for her father to regain his sight. Can this action be called filial
duty? If you were Sim Cheong, what would you have done?

_____

_____

_____

_____

3   여러분의 나라에도 '효'의 가치를 다룬 이야기가 있나요? 소개해 봅시다.
In your country, is there a story about the value of filial duty? Introduce the story.

_____

_____

_____

_____

1장

1 (1) 후손   (2) 남녀노소
(3) 기울어서   (4) 부양하는

2 (1) 손이 닳도록
(2) 대가 끊어지게
(3) 입이 벌어졌다
(4) 무릎을 탁 치며

3 (1) ○   (2) ○   (3) ×   (4) ×

4 ④

5 (1) ① 어질다, 군자와 같다, 마음이 곧다,
행동이 바르다
② 현명하다, 기품이 있다, 마음씨가 곱다
(2) ① 딸의 이름을 청이라고 지어 달라는 것
② 자신이 끼던 옥가락지를 딸에게
남긴다는 것

2장

1 (1) ① 안타깝게/안쓰럽게/불쌍하게
② 생각했다
(2) ① 혹시   ② 아버지
③ 배고픔   ④ 피할 수

2 (1) 어르던   (2) 구걸하며
(3) 알뜰하게   (4) 끼니

3 (1) ③   (2) ②   (3) ①

4 ②

5 (1) 말 못 하는 까마귀도 날 수 있는 힘이 생기면
늙은 어미에게 먹이를 물어와 섬긴다.
(2) 심청은 마른 몸에 해진 저고리와 치마를 입고
있다. 신고 있는 짚신은 다 떨어졌고 버선은
신지 않았다. 추위에 몸을 떨고 있다.

3장

1 (1) 수양딸   (2) 양식
(3) 예의범절   (4) 여의고

(5) 빼어나다   (6) 어푸어푸
(7) 과한   (8) 다과
(9) 장부   (10) 당부

2 ④

3 (1) 입이 닳도록
(2) 마음에 걸렸다
(3) 눈이 휘둥그레졌다
(4) 버선발로 뛰어나왔다

4 ④

5 (1) 심 봉사는 심청을 기다리다 밖으로 나오게
되었고 개천에서 발을 헛디뎌 물에 빠졌다.
(2) 부처님께 공양미 삼백 석을 올리고 정성을
다해 불공을 드리면 눈을 뜰 수 있다.

4장

1 (1) 대책   (2) 근심
(3) 효험   (4) 언약하자

2 (1) ①   (2) ⑤   (3) ④
(4) ②   (5) ③

3 (1) 지었다   (2) 바쳐서라도
(3) 장만할   (4) 치렀다

4 ④

5 (1) 나이 십오 세의 처녀
(2) 소문에 젊은 처녀를 제물로 바치면 남경으로
가는 험난한 뱃길이 무사히 열리고 장사가
잘 된다고 하여서

5장

1 (1) 출항했으니까   (2) 선뜻
(3) 철따라   (4) 광풍

2 (1) 인자한   (2) 이룰
(3) 마주한   (4) 일었다

3 (1) ②   (2) ①   (3) ③

4 (1) ×   (2) ○   (3) ○   (4) ×

5 ②

6 (1) ① 철따라 입을 옷을 꿰매 옷장에 넣어
　　　　 두었다.
　　　 ② 버선을 만들어 쌓아 두었다.
　　　 ③ 갓과 망건을 새 것으로 장만해 걸어 두었다.
　　 (2) ① "앞 못 보는 아버지가 눈을 떠 광명을
　　　　 보게 하여 주옵소서"
　　　 ② "부디 만수무강하세요."

6장

1 (1) 명을　　　　　　 (2) 황당했다
　　 (3) 영문　　　　　　 (4) 터트리며

2 (1) 이별하지만　　　　 (2) 훗날
　　 (3) 맘껏　　　　　　 (4) 나누

3 ②

4 ③

5 (1) ① 말투　　　　 ② 생김새
　　　 ③ 손가락에 끼고 있는 정표
　　 (2) 동네 아이들을 볼 때마다 어머니가 있다면
　　　　 얼마나 좋을까 생각했다.

7장

1 (1) 억만금　　　　　　 (2) 두루
　　 (3) 성대한　　　　　 (4) 풍년이

2 (1) 마를　　　　　　　 (2) 넋을
　　 (3) 난데없이　　　　 (4) 오므라져

3 (1) ①　　 (2) ③　　 (3) ②

4 (1) ○　　 (2) ○　　 (3) ×　　 (4) ×

5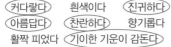
　 커다랗다　 흰색이다　 진귀하다
　 아름답다　 찬란하다　 향기롭다
　 활짝 피었다　 기이한 기운이 감돈다

6 (1) ① 온갖 패물　 ② 시녀 둘　 ③ 심청

(2) 나라의 모든 맹인들을 불러 모아 잔치를
　　 하면 아버지도 찾을 수 있고 다른 맹인들도
　　 맛난 음식을 먹으며 한을 풀 수 있을 것이다.

8장

1 (1) 통곡하며　　　　　 (2) 몰골
　　 (3) 올랐다　　　　　 (4) 간수하지

2 (1) 전생　　　　　　　 (2) 죄를
　　 (3) 금쪽같은　　　　 (4) 저승길로

3 ①

4 ②

5 (1) 싹싹하다, 상냥하다
　　 (2) 고약하다, 뻔뻔스럽다, 무정하다

6 (1) 따뜻한 밥도 지어 주고 집안일도 해 주었다.
　　　 심 봉사에게 싹싹하고 상냥하게 대해 주었다.
　　 (2) 심 봉사가 받아온 돈도 탐이 나고 한양
　　　　 구경도 하고 싶어서

9장

1 ①

2 (1) 조급한　　　　　　 (2) 번쩍
　　 (3) 본받았다　　　　 (4) 두고두고

3 ⓓ, ⓒ, ⓔ, ㉠, ⓛ

4 (1) 아버지를 다시 만나게 되었고, 아버지가
　　　 눈도 떴기 때문에
　　 (2) 심청을 부여잡고 덩실덩실 춤을 추었다.

1~9장

1 (1) 여의고　　　　　　 (2) 바치면
　　 (3) 효심이　　　　　 (4) 제물이
　　 (5) 벗어났다　　　　 (6) 연꽃
　　 (7) 떴다　　　　　　 (8) 칭송하며

1

Blind Man Sim Loses His Wife and Gains Sim Cheong

p. 11

A long time ago, in Hwangju in Hwanghaedo Province, there lived a person named Sim Hakkyu. He couldn't see and was called Blind Man Sim. Blind Man Sim was well-behaved and had a heart of gold, and so the people of the village praised him, saying he was like a saint.

One day, Blind Man Sim spoke to his wife, Ms. Gwak.

"I'm a descendant of a family of noblemen, but I lost my sight at the age of twenty and now even the state of our family has fallen and I'm so sorry to burden my wife like this." Ms. Gwak heard Blind Man Sim's words and spoke.

"Please don't say such things. They say a couple shares one body. There's a reason why heaven sent you to be my match. So please don't think such things anymore."

p.12

Ms. Gwak was indeed a kind-hearted and elegant woman. There was nothing she hadn't tried in order to earn a living in the place of her husband who could not see. Among these, the thing she was most skilled at was needlework. Night and day, she wore her hands to the bone sewing for wages. With the money she gathered through this, she looked after her blind husband with loving care. Blind Man Sim was thankful to have met a wise wife, and Ms. Gwak was thankful to have met a virtuous husband.

But even this seemingly happy couple had one worry. This was the fact that they had been married for over 20 years but had no child. Blind Man Sim spoke to his wife.

"My lady, as we have no children and our family line has been ended, what are we to do?"

Each morning, the couple drew fresh water and prayed before it to be granted a child. And they visited a renowned mountain and prayed with their whole hearts to the Buddha, offering up Buddhist prayers. Then one day, Ms. Gwak mentioned a strange dream she had dreamt the previous night.

p.13

"In my dream, I was sewing when suddenly, five-colored clouds spread across the sky and the house was filled with a fragrance, and a fairy descended from above riding a crane. The fairy wore a wreath on her head and brilliant clothing. Oh! And each time she moved, a clear sound came from her trinket made of jade. But the fairy held a laurel branch and when she came before me, she

bowed. Even now, that fragrant smell and clear sound are so vivid."

p.14

Blind Man Sim listened to his wife's story and then spoke.

"Sure enough, I had a dream just like yours. This is clearly a conception dream that means the heavens are sending us a child."

Just as Blind Man Sim had said, Ms. Gwak was pregnant, and little by little, her belly began to swell. She made clothes and a blanket for the baby, all while praying to give birth to a healthy and kind child. Blind Man Sim also went each morning to the temple and offered prayers of thanks. The couple was so happy at just the thought of a child that they were left open-mouthed.

On a day precisely 10 months after she had dreamt the premonition of conception, Ms. Gwak gave birth to a daughter. Blind Man Sim spoke to Ms. Gwak, who was disappointed she hadn't born a son to carry on the family line.

"More than anything, I'm glad that you had a safe labor. Let's raise this child well and spend our remaining years in happiness." Blind Man Sim prepared a first meal of rice and soup and placed it on the offering table to the goddess Samsin, praying for the child to grow up safe and well.

"Thank you for having our child be born safely like this. Please bestow us with good fortune to have both mother and child be healthy and live a long life. I beseech you."

p.15

But after giving birth to her child, Ms. Gwak's condition grew worse and worse. She struggled to speak.

"It seems this is the end of our bond as a couple. Name our child 'Cheong,' written with the character for clear eyes. If Cheong becomes your eyes for you, who cannot see, then I can leave this world peacefully. And leave the jade ring I wore to Cheong so that when we meet someday in that other world, we'll be able to recognize one another as mother and daughter."

After she finished these words, Ms. Gwak breathed her last breath. It was exactly the seventh day after she'd given birth to Cheong.

2

Sim Cheong Grows Well under Her Blind Father's Care

p.16

To Blind Man Sim, who had lost his wife, it was as if the heavens were falling down above him. But with Cheong crying beside him for breast milk, he could not simply fall into despair forever. Blind Man Sim, who had coddled Cheong throughout the night, heard the rooster crow at dawn and went out to beg for breast milk. Fumbling with his cane to find his way forward, he heard the sounds of a bucket at a well side and women talking. Blind Man Sim approached the place from which the sounds were coming and spoke up.

"Over here, ladies. Please give my Cheong some milk to drink. She lost her mother just seven days after she was born, and to be raised by her father who cannot see, she's in a state where she's apt to starve to death.

If you have any leftover milk that you fed to your children, please give just a sip of it to my poor Cheong."

p.17

One of the women addressed Blind Man Sim. "Oh, poor thing. Since the woman next door delivered a child just a few days ago, I'll go ask her.

"Thank you. Thank you. Thank you so much." Blind Man Sim thanked them repeatedly. After a short while, with the help of the women he had met near the well, he was able to feed Cheong some milk. Cheong, who suckled hungrily, grew full and stopped crying.

"My, the little one seems to have been very hungry."

The woman who had fed Sim Cheong looked at her pityingly as she spoke. From this day forward, Blind Man Sim would go around regularly to receive milk to feed to Cheong, and while it was hard at first, he steadily mastered it. The women in the neighborhood considered Sim Cheong and her father with pity and together thought up a way for them to manage. With the help of several people, Sim Cheong was able to eat her fill as she grew.

As soon as Sim Cheong had grown a bit, Blind Man Sim would put her to bed and then go from this house to that to beg for rice. With that rice, he made porridge for her and was able to buy and feed her the candies that she liked. Sim Cheong grew quickly within the love Blind Man Sim had for her, and one day, she turned seven. Sim Cheong spoke to Blind Man Sim.

p.18

"Father, they say that even crows who can't speak, when their wings grow strong, they bite off and bring back morsels of food to serve to their parents. I've grown this much thanks to what you've done for me, so now leave the job of begging for food to me." Blind Man Sim heard Sim Cheong's words and spoke.

"My Cheong, how admirable of you. But to go out and get food for you isn't a chore – it's a happiness and it's rewarding to me, so it would be difficult for me to agree to your request."

"If my father, who cannot see, should go to fetch food for me and fall down or catch cold, how could I manage something so undutiful? Please, do me this favor."

At Sim Cheong's repeated request, Blind Man Sim reluctantly gave his permission, and Sim Cheong began to go out to fetch food in her father's place. The winter wind tore through her frayed jacket and skirt. Her slender body trembled severely, and with her straw shoes all worn through and no socks, her bare feet froze solid.

But with the thought in her mind that she could help her father, Sim Cheong approached a kitchen that smelled of food cooking and spoke up.

"By any chance, could you please give a spoonful of leftover rice to me so I could satisfy the hunger of my father, who is waiting on this cold day in a cold room?"

p.19

"Oh, poor thing. I'll give you some, so come here and take it."

Each person who saw the young Sim Cheong

admired her filial devotion and gave food generously. With the greens given from this house and that, rice, beans, and sorghum were mixed in a variety. In this way, there was five-grain rice on Blind Man Sim's table every day.

"Father, use warm water for soup and eat slowly."

Sim Cheong put a spoon in her father's hand and placed food from the side dishes upon it, serving him with devotion.

p.20

Blind Man Sim's heart hurt to see Sim Cheong working so tirelessly, but on the contrary, she comforted him by saying that as a child, it was natural that she had to do. And once she turned thirteen she began to take sewing jobs as well, working hard day and night. Thankfully, Sim Cheong took after her mother, Ms. Gwak, in that her skill with a needle and thread was outstanding. Thanks to the efforts of the diligent and thrifty Sim Cheong, once she turned fifteen, she and her father had enough to prepare meals without having to go beg for food.

3

Blind Man Sim Promises 300 Sacks of Rice Offered to Buddha

p.21

The people of the village praised Sim Cheong's devotion to her father until their mouths ran dry. And with her remarkable workmanship and striking beauty combined, word of Sim Cheong traveled through rumor, spreading as far as the neighboring village of Mureung.

The wife of Prime Minister Jang, who lived in Mureung, had heard tell about Sim Cheong and wanted very much to meet her. The woman had lost her husband, Prime Minister Jang, early on, and all of her three sons were living as government officials in Hanyang, so she had expected to live all on her own.

The wife of Prime Minister Jang sent someone to Sim Cheong's house to explain that she wanted to meet. Sim Cheong, who had received this news, spoke to Blind Man Sim.

"Father, the wife of the prime minister has called for me so I'll go out and return soon. I've prepared your meal so please eat first as I'll be late."

Blind Man Sim made a request of his daughter.

"All right, come back safely, and you're meeting the prime minister's wife, so you must be sure not to go against good etiquette."

p.22

"Yes, I'll do so."

To leave her father alone and be out of the house for a long time weighed on Sim

Cheong's mind, but she reassured herself that nothing would happen to his father. When she reached the prime minister's house, a servant came out and brought her inside. Sim Cheong looked at the house that was like a palace and her eyes grew wide. Large trees surrounded the house and gorgeous flowers were in full bloom in the yard, and in a wide pond, goldfish were playing leisurely, making the house unrivaled in size and splendor.

The prime minister's wife heard that Sim Cheong had arrived and rushed out to greet her.

"Are you Sim Cheong who lives in Dohwa-dong? Come in. You're as beautiful as I've heard you to be."

The prime minister's wife and Sim Cheong embroidered and ate refreshments, talking about this and that all the while. The prime minister's wife was very pleased with Sim Cheong's polite speech and actions, and considered her like a daughter. The lady spoke.

"Sim Cheong, the prime minister left this world early on and my children live far away so I have nobody at my side to talk to. If you would come be my adopted daughter, I would teach you to write and bring you up as my own daughter, and I could send you to a good family to be married. What do you think?"

p.23

Sim Cheong was surprised by these unexpected words, but she spoke politely.

"I thank you for thinking of my lowly self in that way. But if I do as you ask in order to make myself comfortable, who will look after my father, who cannot see? I will be

my father's eyes and attend to him at his side for his whole life. Madam, please understand my meaning and do not be upset at what I say."

The prime minister's wife, marveling at Sim Cheong's words, spoke.

"You are a devoted daughter after all. I was thoughtless and asked too much of you, so please don't feel sorry."

After sharing a friendly chat, when the time came for Sim Cheong to return, the prime minister's wife wrapped up some food and cloth for her.

"This is a token of my affection, so don't turn it down – take it and be on your way. Do come again and have a chat with me next time."

Sim Cheong was truly grateful to the prime minister's wife for thinking of her as a daughter. She said she would certainly do as the lady asked, and took the food and cloth and headed home.

p.24

At that time, it was well past Blind Man Sim's lunch time, but he had no thought of eating and waited for Sim Cheong. Waiting inside his room, he heard the sound of the

wind blowing and thought Sim Cheong might have returned, so he went out into the yard and waited again for some time. Then when he heard a passerby going past, he again thought that Sim Cheong might have returned and went outside the gate. Just like that, walking step by step, he reached a stream, and slipped and fell into the water with a splash.

Blind Man Sim shouted.

"Help! Is no one there!? Huff, huff, what's going on!? Oh, I'm going to die! Help!"

p.25

Just then, the monk from Mongeunsa Temple had come down to the village with his offering ledger in hand in order to collect donations to build a new temple, when he heard from somewhere the sound of someone crying for help. The monk, who ran toward the source of the sound, discovered Blind Man Sim, who had fallen into the stream, and dragged him out of the water. Blind Man Sim spoke while struggling to breathe.

"I don't know who you are, but I thank you for saving my life when I had nearly died."

The monk answered Blind Man Sim.

"I'm the monk from Mongeunsa Temple."

Blind Man Sim thought that it was the grace of the Buddha that had saved him from nearly dying. The monk carried the unseeing Blind Man Sim home and asked him, "How did someone who cannot see end up falling into the water?"

Blind Man Sim told the monk everything that had happened up to then. The monk, having heard the situation, clucked his tongue as he spoke.

"Namo Amitabha. Your current blindness is because of a sin you committed in a previous life. If you donate 300 sacks of rice to the Buddha and offer up Buddhist prayers with true devotion, your sight will be restored."

p.26

Blind Man Sim was so surprised at the monk's words about his sight being restored that he spoke urgently, without thinking of his family's circumstances.

"Is that true? Then I'll offer 300 sacks of rice." The monk spoke, amazed.

"Tsk tsk, looking around your home, you're as poor as can be. By what means would you prepare 300 sacks of rice?"

With no consideration to the worry in the monk's voice, Blind Man Sim spoke.

"I would not make a false promise to the Buddha, so hurry and write 'Sim Hakkyu, 300 sacks of rice' in your offering ledger and please have my sight restored."

At Blind Man Sim's repeated request, the monk wrote the name Sim Hakkyu in his ledger and left.

4

Sim Cheong Sells Herself for 300 Sacks of Rice Offered to Buddha

p.27

After the monk left, Blind Man Sim sat still in the empty room and fell into thought. The more he thought of his hasty behavior in his careless promise to offer 300 sacks of rice, the more he found it absurd and regretted it. In seeking to acquire good fortune, he had actually committed a wrong, and was at a loss as to what to do about it.

At this time, Sim Cheong returned home and, seeing Blind Man Sim soaked through, asked with surprise, "My goodness! Father, did you go out looking for me and fall into the water?"

Blind Man Sim was deep in his worries and couldn't hear a sound.

"Oh my, you must be very cold, father. You aren't even speaking. Have you eaten?"

Looking over the table, Sim Cheong saw the food she had prepared was just as she had left it. Thinking that her father hadn't properly eaten and an accident had befallen him waiting for her, her heart felt torn in two.

p.28

"*I left my blind father at home and enjoyed myself alone at the prime minister's house, eating my fill. If this isn't a misdeed, then what is it?*"

Hiding the tears that flowed, Sim Cheong spoke to Blind Man Sim.

"Father. You must be very hungry. There are fresh clothes here, so you change and stay. I'll prepare some more warm food for you.

Falteringly, Blind Man Sim picked up the clothes and put them on. Sim Cheong hurried to the kitchen and prepared dinner with the food she had brought back from the prime minister's house.

"Father, please eat."

But even with the smell of the delicious side dishes, and even with Cheong placing the spoon in his hand, Blind Man Sim could not bring himself to eat. Sim Cheong asked with worry, "Father, are you unwell?"

"No."

"Then are you angry I've returned late?"

"No."

"Then is something worrying you?"

At Sim Cheong's repeated questions, Blind Man Sim reluctantly revealed the whole story. Sim Cheong, hearing it all, reassured her father.

"Father, don't worry. It's no use to regret a promise made in front of the Buddha. If it means your sight can be restored, then we'll send 300 sacks of rice to Mongeunsa Temple, whatever it takes."

p.29

"But in our circumstances, how can we provide 300 sacks of rice? I acted rashly when I heard my sight could be restored, and now what are we supposed to do?

Blind Man Sim beat at his chest, regretful. But Sim Cheong comforted her father.

"Father, faith can move a mountain. There will be a way."

And from that day, Sim Cheong began to offer up freshly drawn water and pray earnestly.

"Lord, my blind father has endured every hardship in raising me, so now if his sight could be restored, even if I had to offer up my whole being for it, I would have no other wish. Please open up a path for us to secure 300 sacks of grain and make it so my father's sight is restored."

One day when she was praying like this with her whole heart, a rumor quickly spread throughout the village that a band of merchants was buying a fifteen-year-old maiden. A neighboring old lady passed Sim Cheong's house while talking to herself.

"Of all the things, in my whole life, this is the first time I've ever heard of something as outrageous as buying a person. And a fifteen-year-old maiden at that! Tsk tsk."

p.30

Just then, Sim Cheong was praying in the yard and her ears perked up. She went out and asked the old woman, "Ma'am, what do you mean? Buying a maiden?"

"Oh, Sim Cheong. That's right. I heard it clearly with my own two ears that they said they'd give any amount of money to buy a fifteen-year-old maiden. What is this world coming to!"

"Ma'am, do you know where those traders are now?"

"People say they have a ship at the dock. Go to the government office and tell them to catch those men."

Sim Cheong said goodbye to the old lady and hurried to the dock. The traders were gathered there. Sim Cheong approached them and asked, "Why are you looking to buy a maiden?"

"We're sailors traveling to Nanjing, China to trade, and there's nothing as dangerous as the passage that we'll make through the Indangsu Sea. But rumor has it that if a young maiden willingly offers herself up as a sacrifice, the dangerous waterway will open up safely, business will go well, and we can make a large profit, and so we're buying a maiden whatever the price."

p.31

"Heaven is saving me after all!"
Hearing those words, Sim Cheong thought that the heavens had heard her prayers.
"I'm fifteen-year-old Sim Cheong. If I offer 300 sacks of rice to the Buddha, my blind father's sight can be restored, but we're poor and couldn't procure them. If you give me 300 sacks of rice, I'll sell myself to you as a

sacrifice."
The leader of the group of merchants spoke up.
"Your devotion is truly touching. Your circumstances are very sad, young maiden, but this is a good opportunity for us, so we'll pay you the price you seek at once. The boat leaves next month on the full moon."

5

Sim Cheong Throws Her Body into the Indangsu Sea

p.32

"At the full moon next month, I'll have to leave father's side, then."
Sim Cheong was sad at the thought of parting, but took strength from the thought of her father regaining his sight.
"Father, I've sent the 300 sacks of rice to Mongeunsa Temple. So don't worry anymore."
Blind Man Sim's eyes went wide.
"What? How did you get that much rice?"
Sim Cheong reassured Blind Man Sim with a lie.

"Last time, the prime minister's wife wanted to make me her adopted daughter, but I refused and came home."

"Really? That's what happened? But what does that have to do with the 300 sacks of rice?"

"I told the prime minister's wife that I wanted to have your sight restored, but that there was no way for me to prepare 300 sacks of rice, and she gave them to me gladly."

p.33

"Why, what gratitude we owe her!"

"Yes, so in order to repay her kindness, I said I would become her adopted daughter."

When he thought about Sim Cheong becoming the daughter of another family for his sake, Blind Man Sim felt sorry and was saddened.

"I'm gaining my sight but losing my daughter, then."

But his thinking soon changed.

"No, this is a good thing after all. My Cheong, who has endured so much until now without a mother, if you can live comfortably in a wealthy family, what could be better than this? Cheong, when did the prime minister's family say they would take you in?"

"At the full moon next month."

"Oh, we don't have much time left, then. But that's alright. If you can live well, I'll be fine even if I live alone. Of course I'll be fine. Thanks to my daughter, I'll be able to see the bright world. And I won't have to live hearing 'Blind Man' now."

Blind Man Sim, not knowing Sim Cheong's feelings, grew exciting. Seeing him like that, happiness and sadness mixed in Sim Cheong's heart all at once.

From that day, Sim Cheong set about making methodical preparations to die. She sewed clothing for her father to wear for each season and put it in the wardrobe, and made a whole pile of socks. She prepared a new gat and manggeon as well, and hung them up so that Blind Man Sim would have no difficulties.

p.34

Time passed as swiftly as an arrow, and soon, the day before the promised one arrived. Sim Cheong couldn't sleep. There was nothing as wonderful as her blind father regaining his sight, but she also worried how he would live alone after she died. And she had said she would sacrifice herself for her father's sake, but death wasn't something she didn't fear. All night, Sim Cheong couldn't sleep at all and watched the sun rise as she heard the rooster crow.

It became the morning of the promised day of the full moon. Sim Cheong changed into clean clothes and put on the jade ring her mother had left her. And then she opened the door and went to the kitchen to prepare a final meal for her father. Outside the house, the sailors had already come to take her and were waiting. Sim Cheong spoke to them.

"Today is the day the boat leaves, isn't it? Please give me some time to prepare a final meal for my father."

"Yes, of course. But don't be too late."

Sim Cheong put her heart into preparing the food and then brought it in front of her father. Facing her father and the table, Sim Cheong put some of the side dishes on her father's spoon and gave it to him, all while wiping away the tears she silenced.

Blind Man Sim spoke up.

"Cheong, why are the side dishes so good

today? It's like my birthday. Did someone's family have a wedding? Did someone's family have a memorial service?"

p.35

Then he spoke while striking his lap.
"Wait, today is the day of the full moon, isn't it? I'd forgotten it was the day the prime minister's family would come to take you away. Last night, I dreamt that you left riding in a large wagon; maybe the prime minister's family will send a palanquin for you."
The dream was clearly a dream of Sim Cheong's death. Hearing this, Sim Cheong couldn't lie to her father any longer, and clung to Blind Man Sim's neck and spoke in a wail.
"Oh, father! I lied to you. Who would simply give us 300 sacks of rice? I sold myself to the sailors to offer myself as a sacrifice to the Indangsu Sea and today is the day I leave. The sailors are waiting for me outside. Father, let me bow to you. I have to leave now."
For Blind Man Sim, it was as if the sky had fallen in.
"What are you saying! Where on earth would there be a father wicked enough to kill his daughter so he could restore his sight? What meaning is there in restoring my sight if you aren't here? Cheong, don't go. Please don't go."
And then he opened the door and shouted at the sailors waiting outside.
"You scoundrels! How can you buy someone to offer themselves as a sacrifice? You call yourselves people? Who would take away my Cheong, who's known only hardship with no mother and a blind father to look after? I don't need rice and I don't want to regain my sight. Leave here, this instant!"

p.36

Sim Cheong stopped her father, speaking.
"Father, I'm the one who promised to sell myself for 300 sacks of rice. It isn't their fault. All I want is for you to regain your sight and live a healthy life. Please, regain your sight and live in peace."
Sim Cheong finished speaking and bowed to Blind Man Sim. And then she left the house with reluctant steps and went to the sailors. Blind Man Sim ran out into the yard and howled.
"No. No. Where are you going without me? Cheong! Please, I'm begging you, just come back. Please come to your father. This father of yours is the one who foolishly promised 300 sacks of rice, so I'll take the punishment. Cheong!"
Sim Cheong turned around to look, saying a farewell to Blind Man Sim.
"Father, please be well."
The sailors saw this and spoke with heavy hearts.
"Having seen Maiden Sim's filial devotion, what do you think of us helping Blind Man Sim to make sure he can live well and won't starve?"
"That would be good."
The sailors brought enough money, grain, and cloth to Blind Man Sim's house that he would not lack for anything. Soon, word of Blind Man Sim and Sim Cheong had spread to the whole village.

p.37

When the sailors were at last about to take Sim Cheong away, the prime minister's wife had heard the news late and sent a maid to call for Sim Cheong. Following the maid, the prime minister's wife discovered Sim Cheong outside the gate and spoke.

"Sim Cheong, I know of your devotion, but is it worth your life for your father's sight to be restored? I thought of you as a daughter, why didn't you speak to me about this before? I'll give the 300 sacks of rice in your place, so return them to the sailors.

Sim Cheong listened to the prime minister's wife speak and then answered.

"I'm doing my all for my parents; how could I ask for riches without a reason? And if I give back the 300 sacks of rice, the sailors' work will be ruined. Even if it's in the afterlife, I'll be certain to pay back your heavenly kindness."

Sim Cheong, who had finished speaking and had tears in her eyes, looked so solemn that the prime minister's wife could no longer offer her any other advice. Sim Cheong wiped her tears and spoke to her.

"Madam, I'm sure you were my parent in a past life."

When she parted from her in this way and turned back to deliver her tearful farewell, Blind Man Sim stretched his arms out and flailed about to follow her, but his foot caught on a stone and he fell over.

"Sailors! Take me. Please, take me instead of my daughter!"

p.38

When he heard Sim Cheong's footsteps get farther away, Blind Man Sim sank to the ground and shouted, weeping. But no answer came in return. Blind Man Sim lied down, buried his face in the ground, and sobbed.

"Then please, take me too. How can I live alone without my daughter? Please take me with her."

The villagers who saw this wept. And then some of them went to bring Blind Man Sim home. Others went to the place where the

boat boarded to see Sim Cheong off.
"Please take care of my father, who is left on his own. I'm sorry to leave without being able to repay your kindness for helping me."
Sim Cheong said this to the villagers who had followed her, and then boarded the boat. Leaving behind the villagers, who could not speak and only cried, the boat carrying Sim Cheong departed the village. Inside the boat, Sim Cheong sat blankly watching the ocean while wiping her flowing tears from her two cheeks.
In no time at all, five days passed since they had left port. The moment the boat Sim Cheong was riding at last came to pass through the Indangsu Sea, the sky suddenly grew dark and thick streaks of rain poured down. A gale blew and a wave rose violently, looking just like a writhing dragon rising up. And then above the boat, which shook to and fro in the waves, the sound of drums reverberated.

p.39

"Boom, boom, boom."
It was the sound of the sailors beating drums in order to hold the ritual. They gathered in front of the offering table and began to pray.
"Dragon King! We make an offering to you in the Indangsu Sea, so please accept it with pleasure and allow us to pass this dangerous waterway safely."
The leader of the band of merchants called out to Sim Cheong.
"Maiden Sim, this is the Indangsu Sea. The time has come now, so prepare yourself."
Sim Cheong staggered toward the front of the boat. She climbed the bow, gathered her hands together, and prayed like this.
"Lord, I'm not sorry that this body of mine

should die, so please make it so that my blind father's sight is restored and he can see the light."
And then she thought of her father and spoke.
"Father, please live a long and healthy life."
Sim Cheong, who had finished speaking, had thought to jump straight into the water, but as she stared at the raging waves, she didn't have the courage. She thought she might faint and hesitated for a long while, but there was nothing she could do. At last, with fear in her heart, she covered her eyes firmly with her two hands and leapt into the dark blue sea.

p.41

"Father, this is how I die."
Once Sim Cheong had been offered up as a sacrifice, the waves grew calm in an instant. Above the tranquil Indangsu Sea, the clear sky opened up.

6

The Great Jade Emperor Saves the Dutiful Daughter Sim Cheong

p.42

The Great Jade Emperor, who was watching all this from heaven, handed an order down to the Dragon King.
"Today, the dutiful daughter Sim Cheong, who was a gift from heaven, will fall into the Indangsu Sea, so gather her up with care so that not a single drop of water touches her body, and after three years, return her to the human world. If this plan is disobeyed in the

slightest, may the Dragon King be charged with a crime."

Thus, the Dragon King ordered all of his subjects to receive Sim Cheong with the utmost kindness. All the subjects in the Dragon Palace gathered and waited for Sim Cheong to arrive. Like a falling flower petal, Sim Cheong's body then sank through the water. The Dragon King ordered for Sim Cheong to be brought to the Dragon Palace. Sim Cheong woke a little while later. As she had fallen into the Indangsu Sea, she thought that she was now as good as dead, but when she opened her eyes and saw herself safe and sound, alive in a beautiful palace underneath the see, she could not comprehend it. It took her some time to believe that this wasn't all a dream.

p.43

Having gathered her wits, Sim Cheong spoke.

"How is it that I've come to be received so kindly?"

The Dragon King's maids answered.

"These are the orders of the Great Jade Emperor, so please do not refuse us and make yourself at ease."

From the maids, Sim Cheong heard an explanation of all that had happened, but eating food more precious than any she had ever seen in her life and being waited on by the maids simply bewildered her. The Dragon King watched over her day in and day out to ensure that Sim Cheong had no troubles during her stay in the Dragon Palace.

In this way, Sim Cheong came to pass a

pleasant time in the Dragon Palace, but at the same time, her heart was heavy just to think of her father living all alone.

"Has my father regained his sight? He must think that I'm dead... Father has fallen into sadness to have sent his child onto the afterlife before him and I'm living high on the hog; is there a less dutiful thing in all the world?"

And then one day, a maid told Sim Cheong that the Lady Okjin had come to see her.

"Lady Okjin?"

Sim Cheong was curious at who it was that had come to see her and rose from her seat to meet her guest. Then the door opened and Lady Okjin entered. She approached Sim Cheong slowly and took Sim Cheong's hand in her own two hands. And then, as she burst into tears she had been holding back, she called Sim Cheong's name.

p.44

"Cheong! Cheong!"

Lady Okjin was Sim Cheong's late mother, Ms. Gwak. In heaven, Ms. Gwak had become an immortal being who lived in the Lunar Palace, and had heard Sim Cheong was in the Dragon Palace and received permission to come from the Great Jade Emperor. At first, Sim Cheong could not understand the reason behind this and was bewildered, but then she realized Lady Okjin was her mother and spoke, deeply moved.

"Oh, mother, mother! As you died just seven days after giving birth to me, I did not know your face. Please forgive my impiety."

p.46

"What are you saying? Forgive me for leaving you so early. Cheong, it's so good to see you like this. Not a day has gone by that I haven't missed you. Let's have a look. Isn't this the jade ring I used to wear? From your speech to your looks and even the keepsake you wear on your finger, you certainly are my daughter Cheong, aren't you? My precious daughter, come hug your mother once."

Cheong went into her mother's arms and spoke, crying.

"Mother, I also missed you so much. Whenever I saw the children in the neighborhood, I thought of how wonderful it would be if I had a mother too. I didn't know your face and so I couldn't even envision you in my dreams, but seeing you here like this is just like a dream."

"Is that so? You did? My daughter, how much hardship you must have undergone with no mother and a blind father."

"Not at all. I'm spending my days comfortably like this in the Dragon Palace and have even met my mother who died, but I'm worried about how my blind father is doing."

In that way, mother and daughter spent a long time sharing all the things they hadn't been able to speak about, and time passed with a cruel quickness so that it soon became time for Lady Okjin to depart.

"Cheong, now is the time for parting with this mother of yours, but soon the day will come when you will meet your father and smile, so don't be too sad. And someday, the day will come too when our family of three will meet again, so let's share our affection to the fullest then."

Like that, Lady Okjin made a final promise and returned to heaven.

7

Sim Cheong Rides a Lotus Blossom and Becomes Empress

p.47

Despite the luxurious life in the Dragon Palace, at the thought of her father living on his own and her mother with whom she had parted, Sim Cheong's heart grew sad beyond compare. On the day that three years had passed since she came to the Dragon Palace, the Great Jade Emperor gave an order to the Dragon King.

"Send Sim Cheong back up through the Indangsu Sea and have it so that she meets her match in the human world and lives a life of wealth and honor."

Thus, the Dragon King prepared a large lotus blossom so that Sim Cheong could safely exit the water. And after loading it with every jewel possible, he rode Sim Cheong and her two maids away, sending them out of the water.

Just then, the sailors who had offered Sim Cheong up as a sacrifice were passing through the Indangsu Sea, having earned a great fortune in Nanjing. The oldest of the sailors spoke.

"It's all thanks to the maiden Sim that we earned this countless amount of money. Now we've reached the Indangsu Sea, so let's give up meat and liquor to the spirit of the maiden Sim."

p.48

Thus, the sailors filled a table with meat, rice cakes, and various fruits and liquor and held a memorial service to comfort the spirit of the maiden Sim. They all felt great regret for having sacrificed Sim Cheong. As they held the service, an enormous pink lotus blossom suddenly floated up gently. With the incredible size of the flower and its sudden appearance floating in the middle of the sea, the sailors were naturally surprised.

"Is it the maiden Sim's spirit appearing as a flower?"

"I've traveled throughout the whole world but I've never seen a flower as precious as that one."

"There's an odd feeling hanging about that flower; I don't think it's an ordinary flower."

The sailors carefully dredged up the flower and loaded it onto the boat. With it on board, somehow, they arrived at their destination of a journey of several months in a matter of days.

At the time, the emperor of the land had lost the empress to an illness, and there was a rumor going around that to placate that sadness, he went each day into the garden to look at the flowers the empress had liked. The sailors brought this precious flower to the palace in order to offer it to the emperor. When they offered the radiant and beautiful lotus blossom to the emperor, he was pleased and considered it particularly precious.

p.49

One day, the emperor was taking a walk in the middle of the night and passed in front of the lotus blossom, and it seemed as if a sound was coming from the flower. When he got closer to take a look, he saw two women standing inside the petals. These two people were the maids the Dragon King had sent to ride in the lotus blossom with Sim Cheong.

The emperor, finding this odd, asked.
"Who are you in there?"
The maids stood on the spot and answered the emperor's question.
"We are the Dragon King's maids, sent on the order of the Great Jade Emperor and the Dragon King to accompany the maiden Sim."
"Who on earth is the maiden Sim?"
"A dutiful daughter sent down as a gift from the heavens, whom the Great Jade Emperor has sent to this world to find her preordained match."
"The Great Jade Emperor has sent an excellent match to me, then. Let's meet this dutiful daughter sent down from the heavens."
And then the slightly puckered bud of the lotus blossom slowly opened and a beautiful woman emerged. It was Sim Cheong. Her appearance was so beautiful that because

of her, the palace was engulfed in a radiant light.

p.51

The emperor called a lady of the court and had her escort Sim Cheong with great kindness. And the next day, he discussed the matter with his subjects and they all thought that Sim Cheong was an empress sent by the Great Jade Emperor, and pleaded with him to take her as his queen.
The wedding preparations were carried out perfectly and in no time at all, it became the day of the wedding. To greet this happy occasion, all the subjects and peasants cheered happily, congratulating the emperor and empress.
After becoming the empress, Sim Cheong made use of her virtuous disposition to assist the emperor, and as she took care of the palace affairs, each year saw bountiful crops and the whole country was filled with song as it achieved an unbroken reign of peace. But Sim Cheong, who had become the empress, always worried for her father in her heart and missed him, and so could not spend a single day at peace.
One day, the emperor, who saw Sim Cheong weeping alone, asked with surprise.
"My empress, is something troubling you? Thanks to your assistance as my wife, the whole country is enjoying a reign of peace. What could make the empress shed tears? Please tell me."

p.52

And then Sim Cheong spoke of all that had happened and shed the tears that she had held back for so long.

"Your wife isn't from the Dragon Palace really; I am Sim Cheong, the daughter of Sim Hakkyu, who lives in Dohwa-dong, Hwangju. I sacrificed myself to the Indangsu Sea so that my father could regain his sight, but with the help of the Great Jade Emperor and the Dragon King, came to be here. Although I've become the empress and live a life where I can envy none, when I think about my father suffering in my hometown, there is no day when my heart is at peace and I've cried secretly like this."

The emperor was touched by Sim Cheong's filial devotion and comforted her warmly.

"Shouldn't you have told me sooner about this sort of worry? It isn't a difficult thing, so I'll give an order for your father to be found."

But the only news they were told was that Sim Hakkyu had left his hometown one year ago and nobody knew where he had gone. The emperor spoke to the grieving Sim Cheong.

"My empress, don't worry too much. As long as he's alive, we'll be able to meet him, no matter what."

Sim Cheong heard this and a thought suddenly came to her and she spoke.

"I have one good way. How about gathering all the blind people in the land and throwing a feast? If my father is among them and I can meet him, my wish can be granted, and the other blind people can enjoy delicious food and relieve their regrets, so it would be a good thing for everyone, wouldn't it?"

p.53

Hearing Sim Cheong's words, the emperor was greatly pleased and praised her.

"That's quite an excellent idea. Gather all the blind people in the land and throw a feast for them, as the empress says."

The emperor's subjects delivered his command all throughout the entire country, asking each person to attend the feast without missing a single one. Sim Cheong counted down the days to the feast as she waited.

8

Blind Man Sim Lives a Life of Hardship

p.54

Meanwhile, Blind Man Sim sat at the side of the river that Sim Cheong had left behind, and spent each day wailing. Even with the offering of 300 sacks of rice that had been exchanged for Sim Cheong's life, Blind Man Sim's sight still had not been restored.

"Cheong, my daughter, Cheong! I must have done many wrongs in my past life. My daughter, as precious as gold, walked her final journey of her own will to have this father of her regain his sight, but your father's sight hasn't been restored and he even lost his daughter, so this place where I draw breath is hell. This is hell."

He couldn't prepare and eat food on his own, nor could he do the laundry or the housekeeping, so his appearance grew so dire that it was difficult to look at him. At that time, a woman called Bbaengdeok's mother, from the neighboring lower village, came to hear of Blind Man Sim's pitiful situation. Bbaengdeok's mother found Blind Man Sim and prepared warm food for him and took care of the affairs of the house, and in this way, grew close to him. Gradually, Blind Man

Sim came to rely on Bbaengdeok's mother and thanks to her, his face put on weight again and his appearance became neat and tidy.

p.55

Bbaengdeok's mother treated him pleasantly and kindly, so that even he, who had felt as if he had nothing to smile about, had reason to smile.

"I'm thankful beyond words that a blind man like me who lost his wife and his child is treated so well. The heavens must have opened up a means for me to live."

In the end, Blind Man Sim took Bbaengdeok's mother as his wife. But she wasn't the good person that Blind Man Sim thought she was. In reality, Bbaengdeok's mother had heard a rumor that the merchants, before they had left, had given Blind Man Sim not just the 300 sacks of rice as offering, but also money, grain, and cloth so that he would not be lacking for them, and she had sought Blind Man Sim out on purpose. Having married Blind Man Sim, Bbaengdeok's mother spent his fortune like water and neglected to look after the housekeeping. One day, Blind Man Sim asked Bbaengdeok's mother.

"Bbaengdeok's mother. The neighbors say that our family's affairs were in fine order, but that now, we're penniless. Is that true?"

"More or less."

"What? More or less? When they bought my daughter Cheong, the sailors said that as I was old, they would make me comfortable and gave so much to me, but where has it all gone that we have nothing now?"

"Where do you think it's gone? It's all been spent."

p.56

"What? Where?"

"I sold the rice to buy rice cakes to eat, I sold the clothes to buy candies to eat, and I sold the furniture to buy liquor to drink. All that's left now is debt."

Bbaengdeok's mother spoke without shame. Blind Man Sim was dumbfounded.

"What? Do you have no conscience? Then again, who could blame you? I was the fool who didn't even safe keep the wealth left to me as my daughter's father. I'm too ashamed to go on living by begging again. Let's leave this village together instead, you and I."

"If that's what you want, then let's."

And so Blind Man Sim, having sold the last of the household goods to pay off Bbaengdeok's mother's debt, put on an empty bundle and left his hometown with Bbaengdeok's mother. A year passed, and the magistrate of the village to which Blind Man Sim had moved called for him.

"The palace is holding a feast for all blind people. I'll give you the money to travel to Hanyang, so be sure to attend."

Blind Man Sim took the money and happily returned home, calling for Bbaengdeok's mother.

"Look here, Bbaengdeok's mother. The emperor is holding a feast for all blind people, so you go with me too. I even received the money for the journey, so don't worry about that."

p.57

Bbaengdeok's mother coveted the money Blind Man Sim had received and she wanted to see Hanyang as well, so she answered that she would. But on the way to Hanyang,

riddance!"

Blind Man Sim, who was all alone, trudged his way toward Hanyang. He tripped and fell over and bumped into things countless times. But whether it was through the help of the heavens, he didn't die, and, alive, Blind Man Sim was able to arrive at Hanyang. On the final day of the feast for the blind, he wrote down his name and his hometown and barely managed to attend the feast.

9

Blind Man Sim Regains His Sight

p.59

Meanwhile, it was the last day of the feast and Sim Cheong was restless.

"This is the last day of the feast but I don't see my father. Perhaps through the grace of the Buddha, he regained his sight? Or is he old and sickly and unable to come to Hanyang? Or perhaps, feeling worried at having seen off his undutiful child, he's left this world? How frustrating not to know anything about my poor father."

Feeling impatient, Sim Cheong thought that she would go out herself to the feast for the blind and look around. Just then, a eunuch quickly ran in and spoke.

"A blind man named Sim Hakkyu just wrote his name in the register."

The emperor ordered for the blind man to be escorted to him immediately. Sim Cheong calmed her beating heart and waited. After a while, a blind man stood before the emperor and empress. As the eunuch told him he was before the emperor and empress, the blind man reclined in a bow and gave his thanks.

she met the young and wealthy Blind Man Hwang. Bbaengdeok's mother thought carefully.

"If I go to Hanyang, I won't be able to go to the feast, and when the feast is over, I'll have to come back and my situation will be worse than before.... If I go with Blind Man Hwang instead, I'll be able to live more comfortably in the future, after all."

Bbaengdeok's mother stole even the money for the journey to Hanyang and disappeared with Blind Man Hwang.

p.58

Blind Man Sim lamented his misfortune.

"Oh, what a cruel and nasty person. She goes much too far. If she was going to run away, she should have brought me to the palace. What am I to do in this unfamiliar place? But then again, this is my destiny and who could I blame? I lived well after seeing off the virtuous Ms. Gwak and I lived well after seeing off my kind daughter Cheong; do you think I can't live without you? Oh, good

The emperor asked him.
"Where have you come from, blind man?"

p.60

The blind man answered the emperor.
"I am a poor blind man with no wife or child and no place in which to reside."
Sim Cheong had difficulty seeing Blind Man Sim's old appearance in this shabby one, so she asked.
"Blind man, please reveal to us once more in detail your name and residence, and all about your wife and children."
As soon as he heard the words "wife and children," Blind Man Sim couldn't hold back his sadness and he spoke, tears flowing.
My hometown is Dohwa-dong in Hwangju, my family name is Sim, and my given name is Hakkyu. I took a daughter of the Gwak family as my wife, but when I turned twenty, I went blind. My wife, who knew only hardship because she looked after her blind husband, left this world when she was forty, and I barely managed to raise the one daughter she left behind by begging for breast milk. But then that daughter sold herself for 300 sacks of rice so that I could regain my sight, and died in the Indangsu Sea. And yet, I have not regained my sight and have only killed my child, and so living like this is no better than dying. Please kill me for the sin of having killed my daughter."

p.61

Empress Sim, hearing this, rushed to her father, and clung to his neck and wailed.
"Oh, father! How is it you still haven't regained your sight? The sailors left a fortune for you; what hardship have you undergone to have grown this old? Sim Cheong, who fell into the Indangsu Sea and died, is alive here before you, so hurry and regain your sight and look at your Cheong, father."
"What? Cheong? My Cheong? Why, are you saying my dead Cheong is alive? Is this a dream or is this real life?"
"Yes, father. It's Cheong. It's your one and only daughter, Cheong."
Fumbling, Blind Man Sim felt Empress Sim's face and heard her voice, but still didn't know her and so he felt so frustrated that he thought he would go crazy.
"Oh, Cheong! I can't stand this frustration! Let's have a look at you! I want to see my daughter's face!"
Blind Man Sim put all his strength into opening his eyes, and as he tried with all his might, he gathered all the regret in his heart and let out a loud shot. But this? Suddenly,

Blind Man Sim's two eyes opened easily and everything before him grew bright. And then Sim Cheong's face was reflected in Blind Man Sim's eyes.

p.63

"Cheong, Cheong! I can see. I can see! I see you, as lovely as a fairy! Are you truly my daughter, Cheong?"

"What? Father, can you really see me? Oh, father! I thought I would die helplessly in the Indangsu Sea. But to live to see you, father, and for you to have regained your sight, I could die now without regrets."

"My beloved daughter. Don't speak again of dying. But what are these clothes and why are you in the palace?"

Blind Man Sim asked this, coming to his senses belatedly.

"Father, by the grace of the Great Jade Emperor, I've become the empress."

"What? My daughter has become the empress? The heavens have been moved by your filial devotion and blessed you with fortune!"

Blind Man Sim clutched at Sim Cheong and danced happily, and the people gathered who saw this spectacle were as happy as if it had happened to them. Blind Man Sim opened his eyes and danced, and sang in a voice that rang out resonantly across the land, and all the blind people in the country heard the sound and all at once, opened their eyes. The blind people who had come to the feast first and had left opened their eyes in their homes and on the road. As all the blind people in the whole country each opened their eyes, another loud clamor went out across the land. The peasants were all unanimous in their praise, saying that thanks to Empress Sim's virtue, all the blind people in the whole world saw the light of the world.

p.64

Empress Sim had her father change into formal clothing and had him escorted into her residence with all kindness. After that, she sat across from Blind Man Sim and for many days, recounted the stories that had accumulated over these many years, and at times laughing and at other times crying, they shared all the affection that they had missed. All the peasants spoke for a long time to come about Empress Sim's extreme filial devotion and praised her, modeling themselves after her, and the reign of peace was without end.

Darakwon Korean Readers

심청전 The Story of Sim Cheong

Adapted by Kim Yu Mi, Bae Se Eun, Lee Young-do
Translated by Jamie Lypka
First Published August, 2021
Publisher Chung Kyudo
Editor Lee Suk-hee, Baek Da-heuin, Han Jihee
Cover Design Yoon Ji-young
Interior Design Yoon Ji-young, Yoon Hyun-ju
Illustrator SOUDAA
Voice Actor Shin So-yun, Kim Rae-whan

Published by Darakwon Inc.
Darakwon Bldg., 211 Munbal-ro, Paju-si, Gyeonggi-do
Republic of Korea 10881
Tel : 82-2-736-2031 Fax : 82-2-732-2037
(Marketing Dept. ext.: 250~252, Editorial Dept. ext.: 420~426)

Price 10,000 won
ISBN 978-89-277-3277-8 14710
          978-89-277-3259-4 (set)

Visit the Darakwon homepage to learn about our other
publications and promotions and to download the contents of
the MP3 format.

http://www.darakwon.co.kr
http://koreanbooks.darakwon.co.kr